The Car Design Yearbook 4

Stephen Newbury

The Car Design Yearbook 4

the definitive annual guide to all new
concept and production cars worldwide

4

MERRELL
LONDON · NEW YORK

Contents

34   A–Z of New Models

Trends, Highlights, Predictions

Trends, Highlights, Predictions

Apart from the 1960s, there has been no other time when design has played such a major role in the car development process. Many customers are now poised ready to accept new design ideas, bored with generic 1990s designs that emerged from customer focus groups. The modern customer is eagerly embracing individual style, hungry for new models such as the Toyota FJ Cruiser or the Alfa Romeo 159. Cast your mind back to 1950s and '60s America, when the cars were distinct and individual models really stood out, and there was great excitement about design in general.

The trouble was that those cars were far from safe – neither the occupants nor any pedestrian unfortunate enough to make contact were offered much protection. And of course their heavy weight made them hugely uneconomical, a price that would be too high to pay in today's greener society. The 1970s saw enormous advances in powertrain technology that enhanced fuel efficiencies, and vehicle safety for the first time became part of the process of car development. All these elements led to a downgrading of the importance of design departments; this stunted creativity, and the more practical factors ended up gaining a louder voice in determining what reached production.

Then the oil crisis in the 1970s created a preoccupation with fuel economy that further clipped the wings of designers and shifted the focus to clean, aerodynamic and invariably lacklustre exteriors. Yet in most respects today's cars are far better than they ever were: they offer more performance and better economy from the same engine size, they are safer both for the occupants and for other road users, they are less polluting and they are vastly better equipped.

Over the last decade, many car brands have merged under the corporate umbrellas of just a few big global car giants. This new business environment has led to a huge push to improve economies of scale in vehicle design and manufacture; for long, the use of common platforms was seen as the best and quickest way to achieve the biggest savings. Sharing components became the mantra, but unfortunately the accountants never considered in enough depth exactly how the products would be differentiated between the brands. This led to few, if any, differences between related models.

Above
The sportiness that threads its way through the Alfa Romeo
brand is clearly expressed in the design of the 159, its new
large saloon model.

Opposite
Toyota's FJ Cruiser offers a fiercely individual style that
oozes character.

Above
For a tiny car, Peugeot's 107 fronts a bold smiling face.

Left
With clear similarities to the Peugeot 107, Citroën's C1 points to a future where the marque offers affordable and cheap-to-run city cars.

Opposite
Despite being made at the same production plant in the Czech Republic as the C1 and the 107, the Toyota Aygo differs in design, as seen in the unique rear door on the five-door version.

But now things are changing; engineering teams are developing ways of sharing platform components while avoiding constraints on key parameters such as wheelbases, track and windscreen position. This in turn allows more exciting designs to be brought to market, and at competitive prices, too. These advances in platform design are enabling an increasing number of models to be developed. This means that differentiation between models is now even more important than before – and many car manufacturers are seizing this new opportunity to be bold. Design is becoming a real differentiator for people: just as in the fashion industry, where clothes say so much about the wearer, the car industry is also trying to offer increased choice.

One major challenge that car manufacturers are struggling with is in the production of small cars. Small-car profit margins are notoriously tight and set-up costs of huge, highly automated manufacturing plants are astronomical. Peugeot's new 107, Citroën's C1 and the Toyota Aygo are prime examples of new models that share platforms and other major structural assemblies to save on investment costs: these three are all built on the same production line in the Czech Republic. Yet despite successful design differences at the front, especially with the Toyota, from the side the three models look largely like-for-like, an effect driven by a common front door and roof silhouette. The Aygo differs most from the other two, with a unique rear door on the five-door version and a quite different styling treatment at the rear: Toyota is clearly keen to offer a stand-alone Aygo product that is not seen in any way as a Peugeot/Citroën derivative.

Car companies have always been keen exploiters of technology throughout the design and development process. The latest sophisticated digital design techniques allow designers to use virtual reality systems to explore many potential design themes, a process that previously relied on the painstakingly slow creation of clay models. Manufacturing teams now also have more experience of how to run many different models along the same production lines. This new and increased flexibility allows vehicle projects to be commercially viable that were previously not possible owing to huge manufacturing capital expenditure; now, running four or five very

different models along the same line can make the extra variety possible.

The consolidation of car companies has now settled, and we have moved beyond the initial rush for maximum component sharing to a new and much more design-focused approach: components still need to be shared, but there are new opportunities for design differentiation. Suppliers to the car industry are also better versed at creating individual components with common mounting points but with different cosmetic styles and finishes.

With this new opportunity for design freedom, the big winners will be the companies that are able to manage and implement the design process most effectively. Design managers must instil passion in their designers and encourage them to connect with their customers, communicating the brand values and vehicle characteristics to the consumer, while at the same time understanding how to design around the physical constraints of different models.

Exterior style is often considered more important from a car company perspective than interior design. There is a simplistic truth in this: unless the exterior draws the attention of a potential customer, he or she will never get close enough to see what the interior is like. The best designs come from companies that enable their designers to dream up new ideas without pressure from sales-biased focus groups. Bob Lutz, vice-chairman and product guru at General Motors, is quoted as saying: "Designers must come up with the 'big idea'. In films, the big idea must come from Steven Spielberg, not from the tabulated replies of thousands of moviegoers pouring out of cinemas." It is this balance between design freedom and customer focus that car company bosses must manage: too much freedom and not enough design critique can lead to a fabulously innovative new model but poor customer take-up – the Renault Avantime being a recent example. Equally, design by focus group can lead to a lack of identity and, at worst, to the brand value melting away altogether.

Brands with strongly graphic badges are beginning to integrate their badge designs into the front end of new cars, rather than simply sticking a small badge on to a traditional bonnet. Citroën's new C6 is a good example of this bold approach: its strong chevron motif spreads outward to form the front grille, making the

Left
The new Land Rover Discovery/LR3 is not only more contemporary in design, but also engineered with a fully integrated chassis frame for better driving performance.

Opposite
Designed at Volvo's think tank in California, the 3CC explores the idea of a dedicated vehicle for three passengers that is electric-powered and features lightweight technologies.

identity unmistakably Citroën. Now with more design freedom, car manufacturers are craving visual excitement and are beginning properly to exploit their brands. This year has also seen a more contemporary twist threading its way into well-known vehicles. The new Land Rover Discovery (LR3 in North America) sees the overall vehicle proportion becoming much squarer than before, and there is a much larger area of uninterrupted solid panel on the rear door, which makes a contemporary statement as it sits adjacent to the smaller rear screen.

There are also examples of brands that have been forced to come up with exciting new ideas literally to ensure their survival. Nissan was close to failure a few years ago but, with the reassurance of Renault behind it, chose to be

bold in its designs. And it has gone on to score hit after hit with the US public: first came the Xterra, which sought to embody the off-road spirit of SUVs; next came a brand-new, modern interpretation of Nissan's Z sports car; and then the pod-shaped Murano and its cousin, the FX, which is sold under the company's Infiniti luxury label. Cadillac has also had to be radical; it has embraced a chiselled-design theme throughout its new-vehicle line-up, and such models as the DTS have helped revive the once-stagnant luxury brand's fortunes. So successfully, in fact, that the rebirth of Cadillac is being used within GM as a template to reinvigorate its other struggling brands.

Perhaps the best example of an automotive brand turnaround has been at Ford's Volvo

subsidiary, where Peter Horbury has transformed the look of the vehicle line-up without losing the Swedish safety-conscious identity. Pre-Horbury, Volvo's design identity was boxiness and utility, a paradigm that came straight out of the Swedish emphasis on functionality that also is plainly evident in Swedish furniture designs. But Volvo's new design identity leaves the unrelenting straight edges behind, instead adding new, tightly curved ridges that stretch the entire length of fresh new models such as the V50. Similar techniques are used in key concepts such as the 3CC, but Volvo has always ensured the changes are not so radical that they risk alienating a loyal customer base.

This skilful brand management has resulted in Volvo's being one of the only profitable

businesses within an otherwise poorly performing Ford empire; it also prompted a promotion for Horbury to lead Ford's US design division. Ford's latest lacklustre Focus is a clear example of a lack of identity, but Horbury promises that Ford vehicles will in future make a stronger and more individual design statement.

Growth areas, particularly in the USA, include the recent influx of generous crew-cabs and utility trucks that now feature sporty styling, an example being Ford's Explorer Sport Trac concept. A new range of more sporty utility vehicles is expected.

Corporate Average Fuel Economy (CAFE) government targets in the USA oblige manufacturers to meet specified levels of fuel economy across their whole model ranges. To boost their corporate economy ratings – and perhaps also to improve their public image – US manufacturers are focusing on bringing hybrid technologies to market, generally on their truck products, the logic being that heavy gas-guzzling trucks offer the biggest savings in CAFE. It will be

interesting to see how the manufacturers go about convincing the American consumer to choose the hybrid truck derivative.

The number of hybrid-powered vehicles continues to grow, and this trend is set to continue. The all-new petrol–electric Toyota Prius is capable of using just 4.7 litres per 100 kilometres, or delivering 60 miles per gallon, in city driving: it has won numerous awards, including European Car of the Year 2005 and 2004 Motor Trend Car of the Year. Within the next decade or two there is a good chance that we will all be driving vehicles powered by an advanced engine – a power package far removed from the simple internal combustion engine now under your bonnet.

It is no surprise that the Japanese are leading the way in developing this technology. Honda and Toyota are currently developing different types of systems that will one day feature in tens of millions of cars around the world. Honda's Insight and Civic Hybrid use an integrated motor assist system that is relatively simple in its

operation, with an electric motor sandwiched between the traditional engine and the transmission, which is either a five-speed manual or a continuously variable type. Fuel is saved by the automatic switching off of the engine when the car is stationary or coasting; assistance from the electric motor under acceleration allows further savings to be made through the downsizing of the engine. The motor is powered by energy stored during deceleration and braking, when the motor functions like a generator to recharge the on-board battery.

The Toyota Hybrid Synergy Drive system, as used in the Prius, is different and more complex. A new type of traditional engine is used, featuring lightweight, low-friction internal components, and designed to run at a maximum speed of just 5000 rpm. A mechanical compression ratio of 13.0:1 improves efficiency, but in order to allow the engine to run on regular fuel, the intake valves close late so that the air–fuel mixture sees only a 9.5:1 compression. A unique, 'planetary' automatic transmission allows a gentle driver to

accelerate from rest up to 50 km/h (30 mph) or
so on electric power alone, adding significantly to
the fuel savings over Honda's mild hybrid results.
Press the Prius's accelerator pedal harder, and
the petrol engine kicks in; for foot-to-the-floor
acceleration, the electric motor adds its
contribution too. The fuel savings are much less
significant at highway speeds, where the engine
must run continuously: this explains why the
Toyota Prius shows up best in the city test.

Other fuel-saving technologies are beginning
to be considered by the industry, too, such as
continuously variable and six- or seven-speed
transmissions, cylinder deactivation, direct-
gasoline injection, variable compression-ratio
engines, and even compression-ignition gasoline
engines. Few, however, promise to top the
hybrid's 25% fuel saving.

There are always opportunities to improve
the design of cars for the future. One widespread
problem is that the A-pillar on many cars partially
obscures the driver's view, often at junctions,
when clear vision is most needed. Increased
body strength has become necessary to meet
the more stringent crash legislation: this in turn
requires modern cars to have much thicker
window pillars than their predecessors did thirty
years ago. An example is the current Volvo V70,
a safe car but featuring a huge A-pillar, which in
some respects actually reduces safety.

The year 2005 saw the Geneva Motor Show
celebrate its seventy-fifth birthday. Fittingly, the
show hosted several models that were a true
celebration of car design. The Pininfarina Birdcage
75th concept, based on a Maserati MC12, was
created simply to show off Pininfarina's styling

talents, and has a giant canopy that moves forwards in a parallelogram motion like the 1970 Modulo, to allow occupants ease of access. Also shown was the Bertone Villa, a conceptual MPV for Cadillac that features huge glass doors that swing out of the way to allow entry to a wonderfully modern interior. Worthy of mention was the Aston Martin V8 Vantage, which is to become a new competitor to Porsche's 911, and which was little changed from the original concept shown at Detroit two years earlier.

So if we really are at a new juncture in car design, the relevance of the concept cars featured in the *Car Design Yearbook* series is greater than ever before. Hybrid technologies are advancing into the luxury sector and new thinking in drive systems will soon make remarkable freedoms in car design and packaging possible. But it is the customer who may face the biggest challenge: not only wading through all the objective technical considerations to decide on a vehicle that meets their needs, but also having to choose just one out of many exciting new products on the basis of what image it conveys and how it projects their personal expression.

Above
The Bertone Villa, one of the more striking concepts shown at the Geneva Motor Show in 2005.

Left
Aston Martin's new V8 Vantage looks set to challenge Porsche's 911.

Virtual Reality in Car Design

Wheel Design

Virtual Reality in Car Design

Over the last decade, the use of virtual reality (VR) systems has become commonplace among the major car-design organizations. These powerful systems allow 3D visualization of digital CAD (computer-aided design) models on a large screen in a darkened room, much like a small cinema. The technique allows a group of viewers to be immersed in the full-size design model so as to make styling theme evaluations or perhaps view a selected design in a simulated real-life environment alongside current production cars.

Car-makers have for a long time embraced CAD as a tool for the complete design-to-manufacture process, but designers themselves have resisted giving up the clay modelling techniques used at the initial design stages to look at 3D proportion and style. These 'clays' are often made as a 30 or 40% scale model in order to facilitate theme selection: once the strongest theme has been selected, a full-size clay can be made. Despite the seemingly limitless power of modern-day computers powering virtual reality installations, the use of clay models is still an

important part of the process of allowing designers to assess the real-life object from all angles in genuine natural light. Even so, the role of virtual reality is unquestionably on the increase.

There are two basic approaches to large-scale virtual reality presentation. The first is a large power wall that has a rear-projection unit, while the second is 'CAVE' (Cave Automatic Virtual Environment). In CAVE, images are projected on three walls, providing the viewer with a sense of being in the projected image by utilizing his or her peripheral vision. To achieve a 3D effect, viewers wear glasses with liquid-crystal lenses. Essentially, the glasses open and shut very rapidly: there is no massaging of the data, but the mathematical models displayed are perceived at two slightly different viewing angles, thereby providing the sense of depth and 3D effect.

Whether for big companies, like Daimler-Chrysler, or for design consultancies such as Pininfarina, a clay model cannot be in two places at once. However, a VR design review can happen simultaneously across continents,

Above
Engineers review a virtual crash test.

Opposite top
A virtual car is used to review visibiliy from the driver's seat.

Opposite bottom
Design theme review using a power wall.

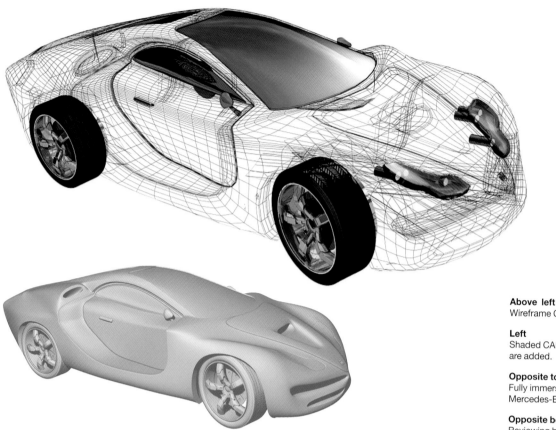

Above left
Wireframe CAD surfaces wrapping the car body.

Left
Shaded CAD surfaces before the material properties are added.

Opposite top
Fully immersed 3D design review of a car interior at Mercedes-Benz.

Opposite bottom
Reviewing headlamp detailed design.

allowing design decisions to be made quickly with all parties involved.

Virtual reality systems are not used only by designers: engineers can review the results of crash tests from any angle, look into the detail of how a prototype car will be assembled, simulate the car running along the production line at launch, or even simulate how a service engineer will be able to perform routine service operations. In fact any aspect of vehicle development that is CAD-based is possible: what is more, all this can take place in the early stages of a project before making the commitment to spend vast amounts of money on tooling.

By sitting in a specially designed and wired-up seat in front of the large screen, it is possible to simulate being the driver – whether driving, parking, or even being in a crash scenario, where the seated engineer can feel what it would be like to have the vehicle deform around him or her.

From a designer's perspective it is also possible to review body forms by light reflection, vehicle proportion and design details. The way a car looks under different weather conditions can be assessed at the touch of a button, as can the effect that sunlight has from different directions. The car model can be rotated and viewed from any angle, with exterior colours being altered within seconds.

Virtual reality is perhaps even more useful in helping with the design of car interiors. Traditional clay models of interiors are notoriously time-consuming to build, owing to their complexity; with ongoing changes to exterior proportions, interiors often run several months behind in the design process. But virtual reality allows interior design themes to be reviewed, with a seated driver able to assess the look of an interior, to reach the controls and to analyse the visibility from within the car.

Virtual reality is not just about viewing new designs on a large screen: it is also possible to create a real-life image of a car in a natural environment that can be viewed on a desktop PC as well as in large VR studios. Real-life environments are possible, too, although there is a complex process to follow to achieve the best results. Mario Malagrino is a designer who lectures at the Florence Design Academy in Italy and who specializes in this technique. A mathematical model of the car's surfaces is built using advanced 3D graphic software. Once the car is surfaced, it can be viewed from any angle and the surfaces can be tweaked as the designer wishes. It is possible to create a photo-realistic image of the car by what is termed 'rendering'. To render a car in a lifelike environment, the material properties of the paint must first be carefully defined in terms of their likeness to whatever paint is to be used. The light characteristics are equally important to ensuring the right balance between light and shadow on the object when creating the photo-like image. The exterior is then rendered to look at the light-reflection characteristics of the bodywork, which may be altered until the designer is happy with the proportion and form.

To view the vehicle in an apparently real-life surrounding is termed 'compositing', which

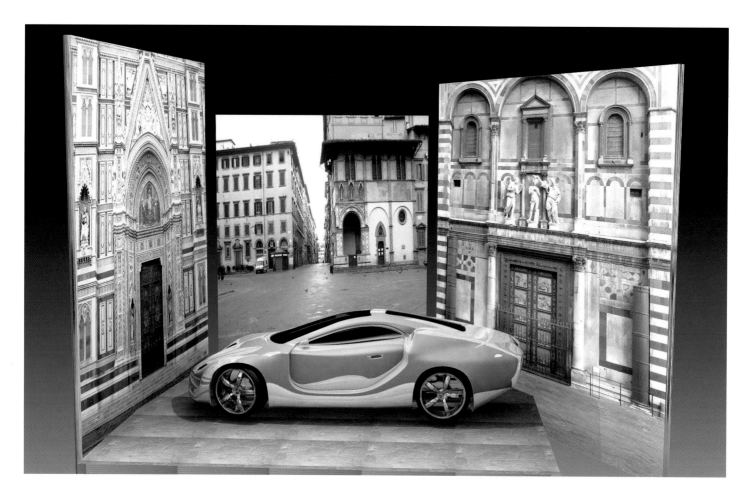

means combining a photographed background with the virtual car. First a suitable high-resolution image must be found for the background: there are no limits on the imagination – the image can be a city square or the dunes of the Sahara. Once the background image is chosen, the car rendering must be adjusted to create the same light conditions as those in the background image; in addition, a colour must be selected that will contrast well. The background image is then imported so that it can be viewed behind the car, and the car is rotated and scaled to the desired position.

Virtual highlights are added next: these aim to reproduce the same lighting as that in the photograph. This is difficult work, as the shadow of the car will be influenced by the light created. Shadow-matching of car and background is then carefully balanced. The next step is to add reflections of objects in the photograph to the car, whether of adjacent buildings or of nearby foliage. To produce plausible reflections, the relevant images are placed on simple boxes next to the car so that they reflect directly on to its surface. The final stage is to add various special effects to give a sense of depth to the image. Among these effects are motion blur and depth of field, which when used together give the illusion of vehicle movement.

The virtual reality process succeeds by ensuring that all the specialists involved collaborate closely, working in parallel to advance the vehicle, step by step, to the production stage. VR technology enables companies to boost product quality and reduce development times – and therefore reduce costs.

The future for virtual reality is in the development of sensing technologies that involve wearing a special glove or even wiring up the whole body with so-called force-feedback sensors, allowing the users physically to feel the virtual image in front of them. This tactile approach will help engineers with such factors as ride and handling simulations, while for designers it will mean the chance to sit within an interior and feel the controls and surfaces around them.

Above
The compositing process involves changing the characteristics of light on the car to match those of the background.

Opposite
Sitting in front of the 'Gates of Paradise' at the Baptistry in Florence, Italy, is a final rendered and composited virtual model of the FDA-Imperial designed by Mario Malagrino.

Below
Light reflections are carefully added to the virtual car.

Wheel Design

The wheels of a car are one of the most important aspects of its design. More than any other element in a car's make-up, the wheels show the way the car relates to the road; most importantly of all, they symbolize the dynamism of the vehicle, graphically depicting its movement as they rotate.

It is hardly surprising, then, that there is such a huge variety of different wheel styles fitted to today's cars. Few aspects of a car's design are determined so equally by both their form and their function. Not only must the wheel and tyre combination look good and provide the visual connection between vehicle and ground, but it must connect technically, too, via the suspension system, transmitting the dynamic loads that keep the vehicle stable and secure at speed.

Whether the car in question is a mass-market Ford Focus or the new Ferrari F430, the wheels are a vital component that must project the right message about the vehicle and at the same time possess the right strength, weight, aerodynamics and cost to suit each application.

Wheels come in two basic types. Cast or forged light-alloy wheels, usually mainly aluminium, offer low weight and an upmarket impression of sportiness and perceived quality; the cheaper pressed-steel alternative found on entry-level model ranges often comes covered with a plastic wheel trim to improve the appearance. These plastic covers frequently mimic the style of a light-alloy wheel.

Light-alloy wheels are typically found on higher specification models to give greater perceived quality and better ride and handling, a result of the lowering of the unsprung mass. The lighter weight of aluminium-alloy wheels means lower rotational inertia, so theoretically acceleration and braking are enhanced. There are downsides, however, as light-alloy wheels can suffer permanent damage by careless kerbing when parking: with a steel wheel, a cheap replacement hubcap is generally all that is needed to make it look like new again.

The casting or forging process allows designers considerable freedom in the style and structure of the wheels they create. Five- and six-spoke designs are most common today, but any number of spokes from three upward can be used. The Mercedes-Benz SLK AMG, for example, has highly attractive sixteen-spoke wheels on its options list; the finned look is a perfect match for the roadster's personality – even if cleaning promises to be a laborious task.

Large wheel-arch clearances used to be necessary to allow for typical wheel articulation when cornering hard or on bumpy surfaces. Now, advances in suspension geometry and more accurate calculation of wheel movements in the wheel-arch envelope have meant that tyre clearances can be much reduced. This clearly benefits the aesthetics of the vehicle as the wheel and tyre fit more tightly into the body, giving a smoother and sportier appearance and with less grime visible under the wheel arch.

On the simple question of wheel size, there are a number of practical advantages of bigger wheels. A bigger radius improves vehicle grip, as the contact patch with the road is greater; there

Opposite
The Ford Focus shows a classic five-spoke wheel with large slotted spokes that is mildly sporty yet not aggressive.

Above
The huge sixteen-spoke wheels on the Mercedes-Benz SLK AMG contrast strongly with the unfussy surfaces of the body and emphasize the power on tap by drawing the eye of the onlooker towards the wheels.

Right
The simple wheels on the Hummer H3T concept look chunky and functional, with the big hub adding to the impression of a strong axle.

is more space to package larger brakes and the ride can be smoother if the larger wheel is partnered with a tyre of similar profile. Disadvantages of larger-diameter wheels are greater road noise (particularly evident with tyres of greater width and lower profile), increased weight and unsprung mass, and the fact that greater packaging space is needed within the wheel arch to allow for a reasonable turning circle. Bigger wheels and tyres are of course more expensive, too.

A wheel must not only accurately position the tyre on the road, as dictated by the suspension and steering systems, but it must also be strong enough to withstand the substantial forces encountered in cornering, braking, acceleration and, if the worst comes to the worst, kerb strikes. As part of designing safety into vehicles, wheels are used to transmit energy. In a frontal collision, the wheels are used to direct energy away from the occupant cell, through the suspension load paths and down into the underfloor structure, reducing interior penetration

and the risk of injury to the occupants.

When designing wheels, the engineers must perform complex stress calculations using the finite element analysis methods, optimizing wheel design for strength, stiffness and weight, within the required stress limits of the various load cases. Aerodynamics plays a part, too: the rotation of the wheel must help draw air around and through the brake discs so as to keep the friction surfaces cool under heavy braking.

So the complex nature of wheel design is becoming clear: it is the joint task of designers and engineers to create unique wheel designs that suit the specific needs of each application. Rugged off-road vehicles such as the Hummer H2 need strong wheels that have wide spokes to keep rocks and mud from clogging up the brakes; air flow and brake cooling are less of an issue than on a high-performance sports car. At the opposite end of the scale, lightweight sports cars such as the Smart Roadster can get away with just three small spokes, perfectly adequate to take the comparatively small forces involved.

Again, aesthetics plays an important part. Wheels for genuinely high-performance applications such as the Ferrari F430 – featured on the jacket of this book – have five thin split spokes to allow a clearer view of the brake disc and caliper, visually emphasizing the braking power needed for the car and adding to the high-grade technology on display to the onlooker.

By comparison, a high-end luxury car needs to convey a message of ultimate refinement, and here again the wheels have an important role in the design. In the case of the Rolls-Royce Phantom – perhaps the epitome of modern-day luxury – the smooth, refined effect is achieved by having a large hub connected to a nine-spoked outer rim. This emphasizes the sheer size of the wheel, complementing the visual mass of the body side, yet the technology is kept hidden as the brake discs and calipers do not show through. The finishing touch is a dark central hubcap engraved with the Rolls-Royce emblem: this balances the amount of visible aluminium. Ingeniously, the RR emblem is mounted on a

bearing and specially weighted so that it remains upright at speeds of up to 50 km/h (30 mph).

Wheels take on a new meaning when a car is moving, turning into rotating fans that provide a direct visual representation of the energy of the powertrain. On certain ultra-high-performance cars the effect is similar to that of an aero-engine fan: the Mercedes-Benz SLR McLaren, for example, has spectacular spoked wheels with vanes that curve towards the outside. This, as we have seen, also has the practical benefit of drawing cool air across the brake discs when in motion.

Finishes on wheels vary according to both fashion and function. Gone are the days when black- or grey-painted steel wheels were acceptable to the consumer. Even on basic wheel types the application of metallic aluminium-look lacquers improves the visual impression, while the genuine light-alloy item may have a variety of finishes that come under the heading of aluminium and which go with most exterior bodywork colours. Surface treatments

can range from high-polished chrome, to matt, satin or polished aluminium, or even a painted finish. The BMW-group Mini is notable for a white-colour option on its S-spoke wheel designs, and the many generations of Mitsubishi's rally-inspired Lancer Evolution have made a trademark of their white-finished wheels.

But the clearest evidence of how important wheel design has now become is provided by car buyers themselves. So keen are customers to add an individual touch by specifying their exact preference of wheel style that car-makers have responded by filling the model brochures with up to a dozen different choices of design. Proof indeed that it is the wheels that set the final stamp on the car's personality.

Above left
The Rolls-Royce wheel is suggestive of luxury and prestige. The two-tone colour adds sophistication, and the outer ring of slots adds rectangular detail and lightens the visual mass.

Above
Highly functional as well as a work of art, the Mercedes-Benz SLR McLaren's wheels act as fans, drawing cool air across the brake discs.

Acura RD-X	Chevrolet HHR	Fiat Croma	Hyundai Portico	Lexus IS
Acura RL	Chevrolet Impala	Ford Explorer Sport Trac	Hyundai Sonata	Lexus LF-A
Alfa Romeo 159	Chevrolet Matiz	Ford Fairlane	Infiniti Kuraza	Lexus LF-C
Alfa Romeo Brera	Chevrolet S3X	Ford Focus	Infiniti M	Lincoln Zephyr
Aston Marin V8 Vantage	Chrysler Firepower	Ford Focus Vignale	Italdesign Mitsubishi Nessie	Marcos TSO
Audi A4	Citroën C1	Ford Fusion	Jaguar Advanced Lightweight	Mazda 5
Audi RSQ	Citroën C4	Ford SAV	Coupé	Mazda MX-5
AviChina Hafei Saibao	Citroën C6	Ford Shelby GR1	Jeep Gladiator	Mazda MX-Crossport
Bertone Villa	Dodge Caliber	Ford SYNus	Jeep Grand Cherokee	Mercedes-Benz A-Class
BMW 1 Series	Dodge Charger	GM Sequel	Jeep Hurricane	Mercedes-Benz B-Class
BMW 3 Series	Dodge Nitro	GMC Graphyte	Kia KCD-II Mesa	Mercedes-Benz GST Vision R
Buick Lucerne	Dodge Ram Mega-Cab	Honda Civic	Kia Rio	Mercedes-Benz M-Class
Buick Velite	Etud Intégral Scooto	Honda Civic Si	Kia Sedona	Mercury Meta One
Cadillac BLS	Farboud GTS	Honda FR-V	Kia Sportage	Mercury Milan
Cadillac DTS	Fenomenon Stratos	Honda Ridgeline	Lamborghini Concept S	Mitsubishi Eclipse
Cadillac STS	Ferrari F430	Hummer H3	Land Rover Discovery/LR3	Mitsubishi Raider

A – Z of New Models

Acura RD-X

Acura displayed a previous design study labelled RD-X at the 2002 Detroit show, but this latest concept is the clearest signal yet of the production version that Acura expects to put on sale in 2006. It is of particular interest as it is also likely to form the basis for the next-generation Honda CR-V to be built in both Japan and the United States.

The latest incarnation of the RD-X compact SUV concept is a far more plausible, more focused and more production-ready design than the extreme 2002 edition. The most striking aspect of its swept-back front-end design is the complex polygon shaping of the LED headlamps. The bonnet drops down on to the fenders either side, running forward to form the grille and rearward to meet the chrome-trimmed waistline. Black trim insets round the base of the body reduce the visual weight of the design, whereas at the rear the V-shaped features on the tailgate draw the eye outboard to the unconventionally shaped LED rear lamps.

Inside there is more innovation and futurism. Ivory leather and suede adorn the instrument panel and door trims, but the dominant colour is bright tangerine-red. This unusually brash shade is embossed to resemble crocodile skin and covers not only the seats but also the steering-wheel rim and hub.

A transparent wing runs the length of the upper dashboard as a truly futuristic statement; large pod-like instruments sit directly below this feature in front of the driver. An LCD screen dominates the centre of the instrument panel and displays information for the navigation system as well as images from the two small rear-facing cameras that replace conventional mirrors.

Innovative and certainly futuristic as it is, it will be interesting to see how much the RD-X is toned down by the time it makes it into production.

Installation	Front-engined/all-wheel drive
Brakes front/rear	Discs/discs
Front tyres	255/50R19
Rear tyres	255/50R19
Length	4610 mm (181.5 in.)

Acura RL

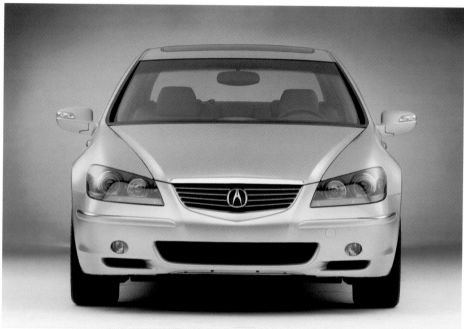

Design	Masaaiki Saito (Large Project Leader)
Engine	3.5 V6
Power	224 kW (300 bhp) @ 6200 rpm
Torque	353 Nm (260 lb. ft.) @ 5000 rpm
Gearbox	5-speed automatic
Installation	Front-engined/all-wheel drive
Front suspension	Double wishbone
Rear suspension	Multi-link
Brakes front/rear	Discs/discs
Front tyres	245/50R17
Rear tyres	245/50R17
Length	4917 mm (193.6 in.)
Width	1847 mm (72.7 in.)
Height	1452 mm (57.2 in.)
Wheelbase	2800 mm (110.2 in.)
Track front/rear	1576/1585 mm (62/62.4 in.)
Kerb weight	1807 kg (3984 lb.)
Fuel consumption	11.9 l/100 km (21 US mpg)

As the upscale division of Honda, Acura is charged with competing with the premium German brands in the North American market. Its offerings have always stayed on the conservative side of the design spectrum, but the new RL, initially shown at the 2004 New York International Motor Show as a prototype, appears to signal a more adventurous style direction. In Europe, the model will be sold as the Honda Legend.

As the flagship of the whole Acura/Honda group the V6-powered RL goes head-to-head with such key six-cylinder models as the BMW 5 Series, Audi A6, Lexus GS300, and Mercedes-Benz E-Class. Not only does it have a formidable array of technology assembled under its skin – including a so-called Super-Handling AWD system that regulates torque independently to all four wheels – but it is styled to create an altogether more exciting impression among its potential clientele.

The Acura designers have set out to create an RL with much more of a pronounced sporting edge than previously. This is achieved with design lines radiating back from the thrust-forward grille, bonnet and headlamps: all highlight the nose of the vehicle and are emphasized by the sloping bonnet. From the side, a gently rising waistline, a steeply raked windscreen and a short boot lid give it a wedgy, fast look.

Acura is going for a younger buyer with the RL, so creating something bold and dynamic was important to the brand. The style is part of this; so, too, is a smart, coupé-like dashboard and plenty of new technology, including a satellite communication system that includes the first-ever US application of real-time traffic information. Also included is a large systems control knob along the lines of BMW's iDrive – and indeed the rear-end design of the RL carries certain BMW nuances, in the way the C-pillar line is drawn into the boot to create a step between the deck lid and the rear lights.

Alfa Romeo 159

Design	Giorgetto Giugiaro
Engine	3.2 V6 (1.9 and 2.2 in-line 4, and 1.9 and 2.4 diesel, also offered)
Power	191 kW (256 bhp)
Torque	322 Nm (237 lb. ft.) @ 4500 rpm
Gearbox	6-speed manual
Installation	Front-engined/all-wheel drive
Front suspension	Double wishbone
Rear suspension	Multi-link
Brakes front/rear	Discs/discs
Front tyres	235/45R18
Rear tyres	235/45R18
Length	4660 mm (183.5 in.)
Width	1828 mm (72 in.)
Height	1417 mm (55.8 in.)
Wheelbase	2700 mm (106.3 in.)

Given that the outgoing Alfa 156 has been one of the biggest successes of recent years for the Italian company, it is entirely natural for its successor, the 159, to reflect many of the design cues of its predecessor and to seek to build on its proven appeal. Yet this is in no sense excessive design caution as practised by some Japanese companies or, until recently, Jaguar: the 159, designed by Giorgetto Giugiaro in collaboration with the Alfa Romeo Styling Centre, is an evolution, for sure, but it brings with it a more solid, substantial look – something that sits well with its many finely honed design details.

Most striking of these is the new front-end design, which, with its piercing triple circular headlamp lenses and large central Alfa shield, is directly derived from that of the elegant Brera coupé – an association that cannot possibly do the 159 any harm in the market.

The trapezoidal shape of the front view accentuates the car's sense of solidity; in plan, the Alfa grille is thrust sharply forward and the headlamp tops sweep outward and backward. The upper body rests on the lower via a creased shoulder line, itself a strong feature, that runs the length of the car. The rear is again an evolution of the 156 but with a greater feeling of weight and presence.

The interior was a weak point on the 156, with poor perceived quality marring an interesting design. The 159 develops a similar architectural theme, including the angled centre console, but the materials are vastly better and the execution much more professional. And as the essential first qualification for success in the premium segment, Alfa Romeo can at last match its dynamic style with a feeling of class and quality that is on a par with the standard-setting German brands.

Alfa Romeo Brera

Design	Giorgetto Giugiaro
Engine	3.2 V6 (2.2 in-line 4, and 2.4 diesel, also offered)
Power	194 kW (260 bhp)
Gearbox	6-speed manual
Installation	Front-engined/all-wheel drive
Front suspension	Double wishbone
Rear suspension	Multi-link
Brakes front/rear	Discs/discs
Length	4413 mm (173.7 in.)
Width	1830 mm (72 in.)
Height	1372 mm (54 in.)
Wheelbase	2525 mm (99.4 in.)

The concept version of Alfa Romeo's Brera coupé was first shown at Geneva in 2002, when its striking good looks made it one of the undisputed stars of the salon.

Now, three years on, the production model has appeared, bringing with it commendably few changes from the masterly original. Understandably, perhaps, the costly and showy flip-upward doors of the concept are dropped in favour of conventional swing doors – but the looks are unimpaired. The distinctive front-end design, too, thankfully retains the flavour of the concept. The grille has been simplified and the angles made less sharp, but the triple circular headlamps are as piercing as ever and the wide and low front-end poise gives it a sense of bubbling energy.

The rear end again follows the concept in its elegance and distinction, though the design is actually softer and more rounded; two distinctive wedge-shaped lamps fan out on either side in a sporting manner, echoing the style of the nose. The rear bumper, with less of a pronounced crease than on the concept, has cutouts for the four exhaust tailpipes and rises to meet the rear screen, which itself is distinctively shaped, as its sides are drawn downward to a central point to focus the eye on the Alfa Romeo badge.

Along the sides, two crease lines run horizontally through the door surfaces to meet the top edge of the rear lights. The upper surfaces wrap inboard as they go rearward, the forward-leaning C-pillar emphasizing the car's wedge profile and its dynamic poise.

In conjunction with Giugiaro, Alfa Romeo has crafted something rather special in the Brera. The mix of mean yet beautifully elegant looks is sure to win the hearts not just of sports-car lovers but of everyone who knows a beautiful shape when they see one.

Aston Martin V8 Vantage

Design	Henrik Fisker
Engine	4.3 V8
Power	283 kW (380 bhp) @ 7000 rpm
Torque	410 Nm (302 lb. ft.) @ 5000 rpm
Gearbox	6-speed manual
Installation	Front-engined/rear-wheel drive
Front suspension	Double wishbone
Rear suspension	Double wishbone
Brakes front/rear	Discs/discs
Front tyres	235/45ZR18
Rear tyres	275/40ZR18
Length	4383 mm (172.6 in.)
Width	1866 mm (73.5 in.)
Height	1255 mm (49.4 in.)
Wheelbase	2600 mm (102.4 in.)
Track front/rear	1568/1562 mm (61.7/61.5 in.)
Kerb weight	1570 kg (3461 lb.)
0–100 km/h (62 mph)	5 sec
Top speed	280 km/h (175 mph)

The V8 Vantage has to be one of the most eagerly awaited Aston Martins ever. When it finally emerged at the Geneva show in 2005 it was welcomed with great applause. Positioned primarily as a competitor to the Porsche 911, the V8 Vantage may worry even the new Ferrari F430 too. As such, it opens up the Aston Martin brand to a broader tranche of younger buyers, the new car being more affordable than previous Aston Martins.

For the first time, Aston Martin now has a three-model line-up, comprising the flagship Vanquish S, the recent and elegant DB9 and the entry-level V8 Vantage. There can be little question that the V8 is one of the most commercially significant cars ever to come from the company.

The proportion is precisely what one would expect: streamlined with an especially muscular lower body and with a relatively high waistline. The upper architecture features a fast windscreen leading on to the domed roof. When the car is viewed from the side, the window glass profile is dynamic and suggestive of the car profile as a whole. The wide, characteristically shaped grille set at the front of the long bonnet is the unmistakable hallmark of Aston Martin; where there may be some doubt is in distinguishing between different Aston Martins, so similar is their overall look.

The V8 enjoys a powerful and agile stance thanks to large wheels set tight into the subtly blistered wheel arches and positioned as far to the corners of the car as possible. This car lacks the pronounced rear haunches of the large Vanquish but has an elegant ridge trailing along its flanks from the air outlet behind the front wheel arch.

Tense, compact and muscular, the V8 Vantage projects perfect power, poise and subtlety – quite simply, British understated elegance at its best.

Audi A4

Engine	3.2 V6 (1.6, 1.8 and 2.0, and 1.9, 2.0, 2.5 and 3.0 diesel, also offered)
Power	188 kW (252 bhp) @ 6500 rpm
Torque	330 Nm (243 lb. ft.) @ 3250 rpm
Gearbox	7-speed multitronic automatic
Installation	Front-engined/all-wheel drive
Front suspension	Double wishbone
Rear suspension	Multi-link
Brakes front/rear	Discs/discs
Front tyres	215/55R16
Rear tyres	215/55R16
Length	4586 mm (180.6 in.)
Width	1772 mm (69.8 in.)
Height	1427 mm (56.2 in.)
Wheelbase	2648 mm (104.3 in.)
Track front/rear	1522/1522 mm (59.9/59.9 in.)
Kerb weight	1550 kg (3417 lb.)
0–100 km/h (62 mph)	7 sec
Top speed	245 km/h (152 mph)
Fuel consumption	9.7 l/100 km (29.1 mpg)
CO_2 emissions	233 g/km

Appearances can be deceptive. The new Audi comes across as a completely new car, yet, technically at least, it counts only as a reskin – albeit a very deep one, extending even to the design of the suspension and steering. Compared with the old A4, every body panel apart from the roof is new; the lines are clean and crisp; yet the changes are subtle in relation to the cost of such massive re-engineering.

True to Audi brand values, this A4 looks well engineered, with the new corporate face, the deep grille encircling black air intakes that give a mildly menacing air. The front styling was first trailed in the Nuvolari coupé study that was shown at the 2003 Geneva Motor Show. By comparison, the rear looks slightly weaker than before – perhaps a penalty of the tail-lamp treatment.

Inside, a new steering wheel reflects the single-frame front grille, and the use of dark grey with white switchgear lettering and crisp contemporary buttons makes for a modern technical feel. Brushed-aluminium inlays adorn the dashboard, doors, centre console and sill trims, with walnut or birch available as an option for a warmer ambience. Further options include Audi's Multi Media Interface. And there is of course the Avant station-wagon version too.

Seat style is based on that in the larger A6, with sophisticated head-restraint design to provide better protection when the car is struck from the rear. Another safety innovation is the 'intelligent' front airbags that assess the intensity of an impact, and in a split second decide whether to activate either the first or both phases of the airbag.

Though clearly a safe design with classic proportions, the new A4 may not be the major step forward that its predecessor was. Time will tell how influential its shape and detailing prove to be.

Audi RSQ

Product placement is a familiar strategy for car-makers wanting to gain publicity for their products through movies and television programmes. But the idea takes on a totally different dimension with the Audi RSQ. For not only was the RSQ conceived specially to slot into a big-budget movie but, as the police car used by Will Smith, alias Detective Spooner, in Hollywood's *I, Robot* (2004), it was also designed to slot neatly into the future, thirty years hence.

Projecting Audi's brand image forward to 2035 meant a mixture of influences for the design team. On a visual level there is clear inspiration from the Audi Nuvolari concept of 2002 and subsequent designs featuring the new single-frame grille. A two-seater, mid-engined coupé, the RSQ features many radical new ideas, the most amazing being the replacement of conventional wheels by four large spheres.

The use of spheres helps to give the RSQ a dramatically different appearance: the spheres themselves are nearly completely shrouded by wheel arches that hug them closely almost to ground level, giving the impression that the car is glued to the road. The four-sphere idea is designed for ultimate manoeuvrability – parking would be a cinch. How they are propelled is left to our imagination.

The gull-wing doors are also eye-catching, hinging at the rear to swing up and open. Viewed from the front the RSQ has piercing eyes courtesy of the xenon headlamps that peer out from under the bonnet. The bumper arcs outward towards the ground, virtually touching it where the spherical wheels rest. The bulging body at the rear houses the huge rear spheres and provides space for large air intakes behind the doors.

Inside, the space is reminiscent of a jet aircraft. Body-hugging bucket seats mould around the occupants, and, to make it easier to get into such a low vehicle, the steering wheel automatically swings into position once the driver is seated.

Concept

AviChina Hafei Saibao

Pininfarina already has numerous relationships with Chinese domestic manufacturers, and this latest collaboration with AviChina Auto Corporation signals a move to link these two companies together in a longer-term arrangement. Under the new agreement Pininfarina will provide design and engineering support while AviChina will concentrate on manufacturing.

Pininfarina has been active on the Chinese scene for almost a decade and has had substantial input into many Chinese models. This experience puts it in a strong position to benefit from the expected growth in exports from Chinese domestic manufacturers.

The Hafei Saibao is a classic three-box saloon with a mix of European styling elements carefully tuned for the Asian mass market. The front-end design has a pleasant, well-balanced look, with interestingly shaped headlamps and some chrome trim adding sophistication to what would by European standards seem a bland offering.

Along the sides are gently formed wheel arches that give a hint of sportiness, and the rear door has a fixed quarter-light window designed to visually increase the cabin area and give it a more considered look. The rear lamps echo those at the front: overall, the Saibao is inoffensive and undemanding.

The growth of the Chinese market has led Pininfarina to open an office in Beijing, and the company expects this will be followed up with new dedicated centres near to its customers' manufacturing sites. While volume exports from China have yet to materialize and few of the products from Chinese domestic manufacturers can yet match the design and quality of European marques, the pace of change is accelerating rapidly and the involvement of expert outsiders such as Pininfarina will soon bring a level of competence to the Chinese car-makers that Western producers will find very challenging indeed.

Design	Pininfarina
Engine	In-line 4
Gearbox	5-speed
Installation	Front-engined/front-wheel drive

Bertone Villa

Although you would never know it, Bertone's Villa concept is based on a Cadillac SRX. Highly futuristic in its configuration, it focuses its design on removing the boundaries between the interior and the exterior environment. The large curved glass canopy enclosing the whole of the cabin is divided into four, each section swinging upward and out of the way on three hydraulic arms. With just a central roof spine left in position, the interior is wide open for passenger access; when closed, a large expanse of glass below the waist rail allows passers-by to see clearly inside.

The Villa takes its inspiration from contemporary architecture where, says Bertone, "luxury is born from minimalist choices". For buildings, the entrance has always been the central design focus, whereas for cars this has always been the front. The Villa switches the priorities and makes the front end simpler and the doors much grander, like the entrance to a special room. The overall architectural look translates across to the large wheels, with their plain covers devoid of ornamentation.

The interior is a place designed to stimulate well-being. The traditional instrument panel is replaced with a wooden bulkhead in the shape of a wave. In the centre there is a large 23-inch screen that makes use of new optical technology and houses all the functions of the dashboard; the only visible switches are on the central tunnel. The front seats are slim and sit on single posts, while the rear seat is a sofa.

To anyone who appreciates radical new car designs, the Bertone Villa is an example of true originality. Bertone concept cars often strive to challenge existing norms in car design: the Villa, though clearly unsuitable for production in its present form, could turn out to be the perfect stimulus for the industry's future advancement.

Design	Bertone
Front tyres	245/40R22
Rear tyres	305/35R24
Length	4900 mm (193 in.)
Width	2000 mm (78.7 in.)
Height	1660 mm (65.4 in.)
Wheelbase	3200 mm (126 in.)

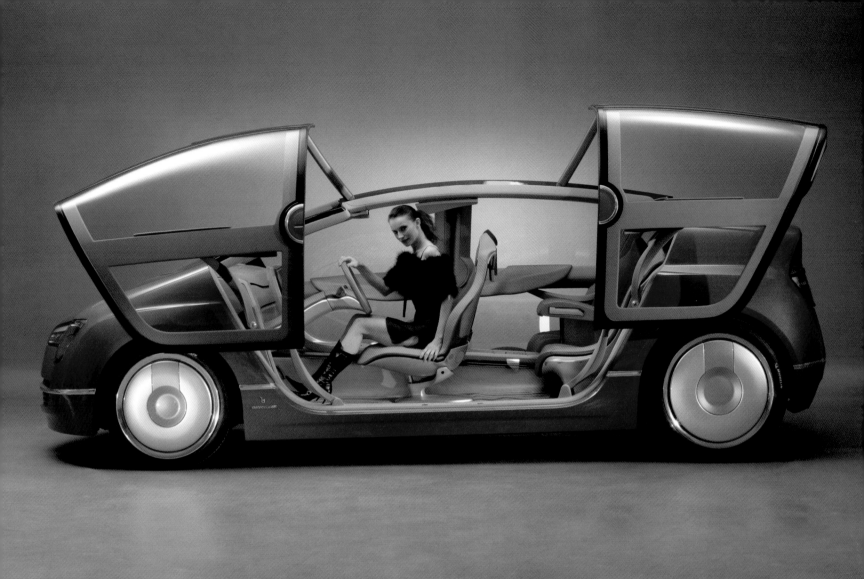

BMW 1 Series

Design	Chris Bangle
Engine	2.0 in-line 4 (1.6, and 1.8 and 2.0 diesel, also offered)
Power	112 kW (150 bhp) @ 6200 rpm
Torque	200 Nm (147 lb. ft.) @ 3600 rpm
Gearbox	6-speed manual
Installation	Front-engined/rear-wheel drive
Front suspension	Double-joint thrust-rod
Rear suspension	Multi-link
Brakes front/rear	Discs/discs
Front tyres	195/55R16
Rear tyres	195/55R16
Length	4227 mm (166.4 in.)
Width	1751 mm (68.9 in.)
Height	1430 mm (56.3 in.)
Wheelbase	2660 mm (104.7 in.)
Track front/rear	1484/1497 mm (58.4/58.9 in.)
Kerb weight	1335 kg (2943 lb.)
0–100 km/h (62 mph)	8.7 sec
Top speed	217 km/h (135 mph)
Fuel consumption	7.4 l/100 km (38.2 mpg)
CO$_2$ emissions	178 g/km

With the 1 Series, BMW is opening up a sector new to the brand – the premium compact segment, with such opposition as the Audi A3, Alfa Romeo 147 and Mercedes-Benz A-Class, plus a host of cheaper models. BMW's aim is to reach younger consumers by means of a more dynamic and more affordable model than has for some while been available from its steadily enlarging line-up.

The latest evolution of BMW design language manifests itself on the 1 Series as a succession of crisp, curved lines that run along the body, defining the edges of gently rolling body surfaces. The mix of upward- and downward-pointing arcs gives a definite dynamic feel, especially when viewed from the front and side. This is led by the clear xenon headlamps that incorporate the indicator, and the sculpted sill, a feature seen on the CS1 concept car and now in production on the Z4. The dynamic features low down on the car visually draw the eye and ground the car as a result. From the side the proportion is deliberately very much rear-biased to highlight the 1 Series' rear-wheel-drive configuration, a unique selling point in this otherwise universally front-driven segment. This unbalanced impression is created by the long bonnet, the steeply raked windscreen, the rear door opening line, and a roof that slopes off gradually to the rear.

For BMW it is a big step – and a definite risk – to stretch its model range downward in this way. But its strategy of going for the premium end in this segment is clearly the right way to go, and such is the complexity and sophistication of Chris Bangle's design that this smaller product can still comfortably share brand space with the luxury 7 Series – and sell in profitably large numbers at the same time.

BMW 3 Series

Design	Chris Bangle
Engine	3.0 in-line 6 (2.0 and 2.5, and 2.0 diesel, also offered)
Power	192 kW (258 bhp) @ 6600 rpm
Torque	300 Nm (221 lb. ft.) @ 2500–4000 rpm
Gearbox	6-speed manual
Installation	Front-engined/rear-wheel drive
Front suspension	MacPherson strut
Rear suspension	Multi-link
Brakes front/rear	Discs/discs
Front tyres	225/45R17
Rear tyres	225/45R17
Length	4520 mm (178 in.)
Width	1817 mm (71.5 in.)
Height	1421 mm (55.9 in.)
Wheelbase	2760 mm (108.7 in.)
Track front/rear	1500/1513 mm (59.1/59.6 in.)
0–100 km/h (62 mph)	6.3 sec
Top speed	250 km/h (155 mph) limited
Fuel consumption	8.7 l/100 km (32.5 mpg)
CO_2 emissions	210 g/km

Now into its fifth generation, the BMW 3 Series has long been the saloon against which other companies benchmark their own products. Yet as a well-established formula familiar from years of high-volume sales success, BMW could not afford to alienate potential customers by changing the recipe too dramatically.

Accordingly, the new 3 Series has been touched only lightly by the Chris Bangle design reforms that have caused such a stir on the 7 and 5 Series. As before, the 3's design is taut and dynamic, with minimal front overhang and the wheels sitting tight in the wheel arches; the glasshouse profile is familiar too. However, the front is more radical, with complex headlamp shapes and a new pattern of grille; along the sides the lines are sharper and the surfaces more in tune with the visually very successful Z4. A particularly strong feature is the longitudinal crease, rising from the front wheel arch, which separates the flat lower side section from the curved shoulder section, and which houses the door handles.

There has been a subtle shift in proportion, too, with a more cab-rearward stance and a longer bonnet to echo the even more exaggerated look of the smaller 1 Series. From the rear the appearance is larger and more substantial thanks to a high edge to the boot lid and high-set rear lights.

A small increase in wheelbase provides improved accommodation for rear-seat passengers, while those in the front benefit from a new and simplified BMW dashboard template, which, again reflecting the 1 Series, relegates the iDrive system to optional status. With iDrive a second hump is added in the centre of the dash to house the display screen.

Technical innovation, as always, is to the fore, too, with the six-cylinder engine featuring combined aluminium and magnesium in its block.

Buick Lucerne

Design	John Manoogian
Engine	4.6 V8 (3.8 V6 also offered)
Power	205 kW (275 bhp) @ 5600 rpm
Torque	407 Nm (300 lb. ft.) @ 4400 rpm
Gearbox	4-speed automatic
Installation	Front-engined/rear-wheel drive
Front suspension	MacPherson strut
Rear suspension	Multi-link
Brakes front/rear	Discs/discs
Front tyres	245/50R18
Rear tyres	245/50R18
Length	5182 mm (204 in.)
Width	1880 mm (74 in.)
Height	1473 mm (58 in.)
Wheelbase	2934 mm (115.5 in.)
Track front/rear	1599/1590 mm (63/62.6 in.)
Kerb weight	1820 kg (4012 lb.)
Fuel consumption	12 l/100 km (23.5 mpg)

Motivated by the desire of parent company General Motors to move Buick upmarket and at the same time strengthen its appeal to younger buyers, the 2006 Buick Lucerne has been clearly influenced by the design of the Velite concept car that was shown in 2004. In time-honoured industry tradition the Velite was used to test the media and public reaction prior to the launch of the already-planned Lucerne, so Buick will feel pretty confident with this new model.

The face of the Lucerne has a strongly featured 'waterfall' grille complete with delicate chrome surround, but nothing so heavy as to detract from an elegant overall look. Lower down in the bumper, straight horizontal chrome bars hint at a sporty nature, and come with spot lamps at their outer edges. The impression is similar to that of the outgoing Lexus GS.

From the side the profile is of a luxury model; the side glass extends back into the gently sloping C-pillar, giving a striking shape to the narrow rear quarter-light glass. A chrome band runs round the side glass, highlighting its profile; chrome also adds a touch of class to the door handles and to the base of the boot lid. One old idea – Buick's once-famous 'portholes' – makes a not very successful reappearance, the four chromed slots on the front fender looking out of place despite being intended to add a fresh edge and emphasize the power within.

The general body surfaces are staid and rather emotionless, leaving it up to the detailing to provide visual interest. Inside, the impression is again Lexus-like, with a wood band running the width of the dashboard to add a warm and luxurious touch. Buick claims best-in-class levels of ride quietness – some compensation, perhaps, for a certain lack of personality.

Buick Velite

Design	Sang Yup Lee
Engine	3.6 V6
Power	298 kW (400 bhp) @ 6200 rpm
Torque	543 Nm (400 lb. ft.) @ 3200 rpm
Gearbox	6-speed automatic
Installation	Front-engined/rear-wheel drive
Front suspension	Short and long arm
Rear suspension	Multi-link
Brakes front/rear	Discs/discs
Front tyres	265/40R20
Rear tyres	265/40R21
Length	4716 mm (185.7 in.)
Width	1921 mm (75.6 in.)
Height	1318 mm (51.9 in.)
Wheelbase	2915 mm (114.8 in.)
Track front/rear	1651/1676 mm (65/66 in.)
Kerb weight	1565 kg (3450 lb.)

If anyone ever questioned the resolve of General Motors' vice-chairman Bob Lutz to revitalize the corporation's designs, then the Buick Velite will put an end to any such doubt. The name chosen for this strikingly simple four-seater roadster came from an élite troop of soldiers in Napoleon's army. Its rear-wheel-drive Zeta chassis architecture is shared with Opel's well-received Insignia concept of 2003.

Buick's designers took inspiration from the company's rich history, while also noting trends in global cultures and contemporary design, especially modern furniture. These have influenced the colour, mood and shape of the exterior and interior: much of the detailing, for example, is in nickel rather than chrome, and gold-leaf lacquer is used in place of wood in the interior for a lavish and romantic ambience.

The long and voluptuous proportions derive from Buick's heritage, conveying power and a sporty elegance. The smooth, sculpted clamshell bonnet gives maximum effect to the bold new interpretation of the company's traditional waterfall grille design, and Buick's famous 'portholes' adorn the front wings. The stance of the Velite is certainly impressive, particularly from the rear, where large, high-set tail lamps complement the boat-tail effect of the raised arc that runs in the sheet metal back from the A-pillars. The folding soft-top is covered by a clamshell lid when stowed.

The side of the car is barrelled inward slightly, so that light from above creates gradually darkening shades as it moves downward, finally brightening as it hits the ridge towards the bottom of the door.

This is an inviting design in so many ways, and the interior is no exception. The cockpit design mixes contemporary and retro styling themes, with brown-faced, nickel-rimmed instruments and iceberg-blue leather. "A new expression of American premium style" is how Buick very temptingly bills it.

Cadillac BLS

Design	Chip Thole
Engine	2.8 V6 (2.0 in-line 4, and 1.9 diesel, also offered)
Installation	Front-engined/front-wheel drive
Front suspension	MacPherson strut
Rear suspension	Multi-link
Brakes front/rear	Discs/discs
Length	4680 mm (184.3 in.)
Width	1762 mm (69.4 in.)
Height	1449 mm (57 in.)

The BLS marks many firsts for Cadillac. A medium-size saloon designed to compete with the likes of the BMW 3 Series, it is the first Cadillac to be sold exclusively in Europe, where the car is due for launch in the spring of 2006. Unusually, it is built in Europe, too – in Sweden, to be precise, as it is based on the front-wheel-drive architecture of the Saab 9-3.

But while the origins of the BLS might be unconventional and the Cadillac name somewhat unfamiliar in Europe, the crisp design language that defines all new Cadillacs will strike a chord with transatlantic travellers or, for that matter, anyone who watches American television. Cadillac's well-established, sharply defined contours and striking wedge-shaped proportions will make the BLS stand out from the crowd. The characteristic crosshatched grille and chunky headlamps are impressive in their boldness but work well on the smaller silhouette of the BLS, while at the rear the vertical lights – again oversized – and long central stop-light are distinctive and dramatic. The effect is bold and clearly American, but stops short of the kind of brashness that might alienate the European customer.

Running across the front and rear ends is a centre crease that adds interest to the large, otherwise featureless surfaces. From the side the silhouette is strong, too, the doors being the only body panels shared with the Saab.

Inside, the cockpit design is clearly differentiated from the Saab donor car, with a black upper dashboard featuring brushed-aluminium highlights and a somewhat incongruous rectangular analogue clock, a feature shared with the large Cadillac DTS. The three-spoke steering wheel is a carryover from the Saab.

Overall, the BLS has good proportions and strong detailing and could at last give Cadillac a genuine competitor with which to challenge the all-powerful clique of European premium saloons.

Cadillac DTS

Engine	4.6 V8
Power	217 kW (291 bhp) @ 5600 rpm
Torque	388 Nm (286 lb. ft.) @ 4400 rpm
Gearbox	4-speed automatic
Installation	Front-engined/rear-wheel drive
Front suspension	MacPherson strut
Rear suspension	Multi-link
Brakes front/rear	Discs/discs
Front tyres	245/45R18
Rear tyres	245/45R18
Length	5274 mm (207.6 in.)
Width	1901 mm (74.8 in.)
Height	1464 mm (57.6 in.)
Wheelbase	2936 mm (115.6 in.)
Track front/rear	1591/1580 mm (62.6/62.2 in.)
Fuel consumption	10.7 l/100 km (22 US mpg)

As the flagship of the line-up, and due to replace the iconic DeVille in the autumn of 2005, the new DTS is perhaps the most important Cadillac of them all: so important, in fact, that it was previewed by no less a figure than President Bush at his inauguration for his second term in 2005.

The DTS brings this American national institution up to date with the adoption of Cadillac's new chiselled design language; it does nothing to hide its size and, some might say, vulgarity. The new design stays faithful to the classic three-box proportions of old American full-size cars, with the long flat bonnet and boot lid accentuated by the steeply rising windscreen and falling rear screen, themselves giving rise to distinct corners at the tops of the A- and C-pillars.

At more than 5 metres (16 ft.) in length and with its huge grille and headlamps, the sheer size of this car gives it an amazing presence – one that oozes both attitude and power. From whichever angle you look at the DTS, vast size and status is the clear message portrayed. At the rear a massively wide boot lid extends out to narrow vertical rear lamps, again accentuating width.

Unashamedly large and sumptuous, the DTS's interior has left behind the ornate, chintzy and over-complex treatment of earlier Cadillacs; instead, the approach taken here is much calmer, cleaner and more Lexus-like. A large central screen dominates proceedings; a perhaps intentionally provocative touch is the square clock that contrasts with the circular instrument dials.

Whatever one's view of the big Cadillac's style, its proportions and its detailed execution, it certainly does not suffer from a lack of identity – a frequent complaint about large Japanese models. On the contrary, the DTS could find itself celebrated as a symbol of American design in 2005.

Cadillac STS

Engine	4.6 V8 (3.6 V6 also offered)
Power	239 kW (320 bhp) @ 6400 rpm
Torque	427 Nm (315 lb. ft.) @ 4400 rpm
Gearbox	5-speed automatic
Installation	Front-engined/rear-wheel drive or all-wheel drive
Front suspension	Independent short and long arm
Rear suspension	Multi-link
Brakes front/rear	Discs/discs
Front tyres	235/50R18
Rear tyres	255/45R18
Length	4986 mm (196.3 in.)
Width	1844 mm (72.6 in.)
Height	1463 mm (57.6 in.)
Wheelbase	2956 mm (116.4 in.)
Track front/rear	1569/1581 mm (61.8/62.2 in.)
Kerb weight	1779 kg (3922 lb.)
0–100 km/h (62 mph)	6 sec
Fuel consumption	9.4 l/100 km (24 US mpg)

The Cadillac STS replaces the Seville, the luxury saloon that was introduced in 1956 as a limited-production model of the Eldorado, and which went on to become the US luxury brand's staple product. The STS is the latest of a new generation of rear-wheel-drive Cadillacs and is based on the General Motors Sigma chassis architecture. As such, this new model squarely targets the luxury end of the sophisticated American market.

The STS uses styling cues that are found throughout the new-era Cadillac range, especially the smaller CTS: the new angular design language gives the modern Cadillac brand a strong design identity. This chiselled, contemporary look mixes flat surfaces and straight lines with strong creases and sharp corners to maximum effect, but without leaving the whole car looking too boxy or unconsidered. The overall impression remains of a solid-looking and well-engineered machine.

Compared to its smaller brother, the CTS, the new STS has a more steeply raked windscreen, a lower roofline and a closer wheel-to-wheel-arch relationship. The vertical headlamps remain but are slightly narrower and lower than the style seen on other cars in the range. At the rear, LED tail lamps are designed with indirect optics to improve the perceived quality of the light.

The interior has a businesslike look to it, with restrained graphics and clean overall architecture. Eucalyptus wood is used on the top section of the steering-wheel rim, the centre console, the instrument panel and the door armrests, creating a clear contrast with the pale-grey and beige trim. Next-generation technology is discreet but impressive, with remote engine start from 60 metres (200 feet) away, an automatic cruise control that adapts to the speed of cars in front, projector beam headlamps that automatically switch between high and low beams, and 150-command voice recognition.

Chevrolet HHR

The Chevrolet HHR has puzzled many within the car business, not just with the unashamed nostalgia of its design, but also by virtue of the fact that it has appeared well after those first retro hits, the Chrysler PT Cruiser and the VW Beetle, have faded in the sales charts and Ford has been criticized for the excessively rear-view-mirror nature of much of its design output.

Perhaps for this very reason Chevrolet presented an immediate parallel modern take on the HHR's retro theme, in the shape of a version customized by West Coast Customs, the firm behind the popular *Pimp my Ride* television show. The HHR draws on styling themes from the 1949 Chevy Suburban and the more modern SSR roadster. More of a station-wagon than the PT Cruiser, the HHR features boxy and deep flared wheel arches that jut from the body and make a clear anti-aerodynamic design statement – almost as if the HHR should be best appreciated stationary rather than on the highway. At the front the one-piece, bulging metal hood recalls the '49 Suburban heritage and sends a feature line up the A-pillar and a sharper crease along into the doors, confirming that this car has modern features too.

The lamps at the front have the effect of widening and grounding the HHR, while the large chrome grille suggests power beneath – perhaps more so than one would expect for only 170 bhp. Small round lights at the rear complement the retro look and allow more space for a wide tailgate. Inside, the high roofline gives an unusual feeling of space, and a commanding driving position allows great visibility. But while the HHR is clearly roomy and practical, its ultimate success will still depend on the American buyer's continuing appetite for nostalgia.

Engine	2.4 in-line 4 (2.2 also offered)
Power	127 kW (170 bhp) @ 6000 rpm
Torque	230 Nm (170 lb. ft.) @ 4400 rpm
Gearbox	5-speed manual
Installation	Front-engined/front-wheel drive
Front suspension	MacPherson strut
Rear suspension	Semi-independent torsion beam
Brakes front/rear	Discs/drums
Length	4432 mm (174.5 in.)
Width	1730 mm (68.1 in.)
Height	1562 mm (61.5 in.)
Wheelbase	2620 mm (103.2 in.)

Chevrolet Impala

Engine	5.3 V8 (3.5 and 3.9 V6 also offered)
Power	226 kW (303 bhp) @ 5600 rpm
Torque	438 Nm (323 lb. ft.) @ 4400 rpm
Gearbox	4-speed automatic
Installation	Front-engined/front-wheel drive
Front suspension	MacPherson strut
Rear suspension	Tri-link
Brakes front/rear	Discs/discs
Front tyres	P235/50R18
Rear tyres	P235/50R18
Length	5091 mm (200.4 in.)
Width	1851 mm (72.9 in.)
Height	1487 mm (58.5 in.)
Wheelbase	2807 mm (110.5 in.)
Track front/rear	1585/1562 mm (62.4/61.5 in.)

The Impala is one of the most famous Chevrolet nameplates, and the most recent edition has sold more than one million units since its launch in 1999; the more sporty-looking Monte Carlo coupé derivative has its roots in NASCAR racing.

For the 2006 model year the Impala has undergone a complete redesign. However, the new car's exterior appearance is disappointingly bland, with a front-end design that lacks presence. The headlamps have a premium look but the upper grille and front edge of the bonnet appear weak by comparison. From the side there are chunky door handles and a chrome trim that runs round the side windows, enhancing – albeit in a token way – the luxury look. At the rear the lines of the boot and lamps are clean and contemporary but there is something slightly uncomfortable about the contrast between the upper planar surfaces and the bulging rear bumper.

A technology enhancement worthy of mention at the front is the new design of windscreen wiper: a flat blade is able to give constant pressure on the glass, helping to eliminate streaking and wind noise.

The new models are available with a new V8 engine featuring GM's 'displacement on demand' technology that automatically switches between eight- and four-cylinder power. The idea is that the engine uses only as many cylinders as the driving situation demands: the result is up to 12% improved fuel economy.

Inside there is subtle innovation with a flip-and-fold rear seat where the rear seat cushions hide a covered storage area underneath. The seat back can also be folded flat to make an open space for long luggage.

In contrast to some of its predecessors, this Impala is no design sensation. Nevertheless, its unobtrusive looks, keen price and large size will ensure it a broad market.

Production

Chevrolet Matiz

Design	Italdesign/Chevrolet
Engine	1.0 in-line 4
Power	48 kW (65 bhp) @ 5400 rpm
Torque	91 Nm (67 lb. ft.) @ 4200 rpm
Gearbox	5-speed
Installation	Front-engined/front-wheel drive
Front suspension	MacPherson strut
Rear suspension	Torsion beam
Brakes front/rear	Discs/drums
Front tyres	155/65R13
Rear tyres	155/65R13
Length	3495 mm (137.6 in.)
Width	1494 mm (58.8 in.)
Height	1500 mm (59 in.)
Wheelbase	2344 mm (92.3 in.)
Track front/rear	1311/1275 mm (51.6/50.2 in.)
Kerb weight	795 kg (1753 lb.)
0–100 km/h (62 mph)	14.1 sec (est.)
Top speed	156 km/h (97 mph)
Fuel consumption	5.6 l/100 km (50.4 mpg)
CO_2 emissions	139 g/km

The designation of the M3X 'concept' shown at the 2004 Paris salon might have been unfamiliar but the shape was not. The tiny concept marked the start of something big for Chevrolet, which in General Motors' new European strategy has become the entry-level brand for the group in Europe, with a line-up of small and mid-size vehicles sourced from Daewoo in low-cost Korea. Opel-Vauxhall and Saab will now offer European-built models with greater sophistication at a correspondingly higher quality and price point.

The M3X looked familiar for the very simple reason that it was no more than a face-lift of the Daewoo Matiz, the already successful micro that is the mainstay of the budget category in every European car rental fleet. But while Daewoos are now smartly rebranded as Chevrolets, not every model is as new as it looks, and the M3X's Matiz platform dates back to 1998; competitors are thus technically more up to date. That said, Chevrolet's revamp of Italdesign's original design, launched at Geneva in 2005, is clever and attractive. The new version of the Matiz has the same narrow proportions, but a friendly face with cheerful LED headlamps that dominate the front; at the rear, bold, fun-looking circular lights intersect the tailgate, rear screen and body side panel.

The interior is simple and playful, done out in a two-tone colour scheme that uses the body colour – often bright – and black; the most notable improvement brought in with the switch to Chevrolet is the central instrument pack containing the principal displays.

The rebranding programme for Chevrolet Europe is a costly and complex one. The name has been successful on small cars in South America – so GM is clearly counting on the European mass market to show the same willingness to readjust its ideas of what a Chevrolet can be.

Chevrolet S3X

General Motors decided in the autumn of 2004 to use products from its Daewoo Corporation in South Korea to gain it competitive advantage in the many segments of the European market where value for money, rather than nameplate prestige, is the most important factor. The cars would be branded Chevrolet, and this attractive concept was developed to provide potential buyers with a clear idea of the exciting ideas that were in store for the new-to-Europe marque.

The S3X is a freshly styled concept for a seven-seater family vehicle that is a crossover between a four-wheel-drive SUV, a smart station-wagon and a people-carrier. The concept is similar in length and width to a Mercedes-Benz ML-Class and, with plenty of ground clearance thanks to 20-inch wheels and big wheel arches, it clearly spells out its off-road intentions. A tough plastic skirt complete with aluminium skidplates protects the body from stone chips and reinforces the rugged look.

The exterior is well judged for Europe. Crisp feature lines adorn the sides and rear, with the front using softer radii to portray a friendlier face. The roof is made up of six large louvred glass panels that can slide rearward to create a long opening. Overall, there is a good balance between practical workhorse and plush executive car, a combination the market seems to like. Such features as the separately hinged rear window and the two rows of fold-flat rear seats suggest a further role as a versatile family people-carrier in the mould of the Opel Zafira, one of GM's few really big European successes.

When the S3X launches in 2006 it will be the first product to have been entirely conceived under GM's ownership of Daewoo – and its quality and refinement as well as its design and price will come under close scrutiny.

Installation	Front-engined/four-wheel drive
Brakes front/rear	Discs/discs
Front tyres	20 in.
Rear tyres	20 in.
Length	4639 mm (182.6 in.)
Width	1848 mm (72.8 in.)
Height	1722 mm (67.8 in.)
Wheelbase	2700 mm (106.3 in.)

Chrysler Firepower

Design	Brandon Faurote/Trevor Creed
Engine	6.1 V8
Power	317 kW (425 bhp)
Gearbox	5-speed automatic
Installation	Front-engined/rear-wheel drive
Front suspension	Double wishbone
Rear suspension	Double wishbone
Brakes front/rear	Discs/discs
Front tyres	275/35R19
Rear tyres	335/30R20
Length	4383 mm (172.6 in.)
Width	1859 mm (73.2 in.)
Height	1211 mm (47.7 in.)
Wheelbase	2510 mm (98.8 in.)
Track front/rear	1565/1539 mm (61.6/60.6 in.)
Kerb weight	1533 kg (3380 lb.)
0–100 km/h (62 mph)	4.5 sec
Top speed	282 km/h (175 mph)

While the Firepower name might immediately suggest the ultimate in no-holds-barred performance, Chrysler is quick to point out that this concept is a grand tourer rather than an out-and-out sports car – not least because it is too heavy and too highly specified to be nimble like a Ferrari 360. Instead, say Chrysler designers, the Firepower should be seen as a bridge between the current Crossfire and the much more extreme ME Four-Twelve supercar prototype shown in 2004.

The large rectangular grille, set low beneath the line of the piercing headlamps, presents an unnerving front-end design that becomes stronger still as the body wraps rearward to the massive carved rear wheel arches. From the rear the emphasis is on width and power, with carbon-fibre trim encasing the exhausts. From this angle there is also more than a hint of the new Aston Martin DB9.

The sumptuous and rich interior mixes very dark blue leather with what Chrysler describes as oyster leather and behr maple accents. Large expanses of chrome give the Firepower cabin a distinctly sumptuous and American identity, making for a clear contrast with the more technical feel of equivalent European designs.

A 6.1-litre Hemi engine and a Dodge Viper-based chassis ensure that the Firepower will win no awards for environmental responsibility, let alone relevance to the everyday buyer. Instead, the model's role is one of a flag-flyer for the Chrysler marque and its aspirations to be seen as a sophisticated and refined brand worthy of being mentioned in the same breath as thoroughbred European designs as well as American muscle cars. Stylistically, at least, the Firepower comes across as Chrysler's answer to the Aston Martin Vanquish – and that must mean it has succeeded in its mission.

Citroën C1

Engine	1.0 in-line 3 (1.4 in-line 4 diesel also offered)
Power	51 kW (68 bhp) @ 6000 rpm
Torque	93 Nm (68 lb. ft.) @ 3600 rpm
Gearbox	5-speed manual
Installation	Front-engined/front-wheel drive
Front suspension	MacPherson strut
Rear suspension	Torsion beam
Brakes front/rear	Discs/drums
Front tyres	155/65R14
Rear tyres	155/65R14
Length	3430 mm (135 in.)
Width	1630 mm (64.2 in.)
Height	1460 mm (57.5 in.)
Wheelbase	2340 mm (92.1 in.)
Kerb weight	790 kg (1742 lb.)
0–100 km/h (62 mph)	13.7 sec
Top speed	157 km/h (98 mph)
Fuel consumption	4.6 l/100 km (61.4 mpg)

With Citroën, Peugeot and Toyota collaborating to conceive and build a new low-cost, entry-level small car – one for each company – the three firms' designers faced a significant challenge: how to give each brand's offering a distinct visual identity, yet keep the maximum number of components the same so as to reduce parts costs and simplify manufacture.

The general consensus must be that those designers have succeeded very well. Anyone seeking a low-cost, fun-looking runabout need look no further than the trio from the Kolin factory in the Czech Republic. Like its peers from Peugeot (the 107) and Toyota (the Aygo), the new Citroën C1 is a cheerful, compact city car with a keen personality.

The front end is bright and youthful, with large headlamps and a smiling face. A sporty appearance is highlighted by the wheels pushed right to the corners, especially at the rear where the close body-to-wheel relationship is similar to that of the iconic Smart. The rear quarter-window on the three-door version kicks up into the big C-pillar to add visual strength; the side treatment on the five-door is innovative, with the rear doors extending back to meet the tail lights, thus simplifying the C1's appearance as well as its assembly.

The tailgate is innovative, too: it is entirely glass and extends down below the lamps. The interior is deliberately playful in nature, with a chunky circular speedometer in front of the driver and a separate 'add-on' rev counter in the style of the Mini; the air vents are ball-shaped, the controls simple and the steering wheel a sporty three-spoke.

The C1 will compete in the market not just with such familiar opponents as the Fiat Panda and the Ford Ka, but also with the Peugeot and Toyota models produced alongside it; for customers, therefore, the choice will come down to style and nothing else.

Citroën C4

Engine	2.0 in-line 4 (1.4 and 1.6, and 1.6 and 2.0 diesel, also offered)
Power	103 kW (138 bhp) @ 6000 rpm
Torque	190 Nm (140 lb. ft.) @ 4100 rpm
Gearbox	5-speed manual
Installation	Front-engined/front-wheel drive
Front suspension	MacPherson strut
Rear suspension	Trailing arm
Brakes front/rear	Discs/discs
Front tyres	205/50R17
Rear tyres	205/50R17
Length	4274 mm (168.3 in.)
Width	1769 mm (69.7 in.)
Height	1458 mm (57.4 in.)
Wheelbase	2608 mm (102.7 in.)
Track front/rear	1497/1502 mm (58.9/59.1 in.)
Kerb weight	1262 kg (2782 lb.)
0–100 km/h (62 mph)	9.2 sec
Top speed	207 km/h (129 mph)
Fuel consumption	7.8 l/100 km (36.2 mpg)
CO$_2$ emissions	186 g/km

The C4 has been welcomed with open arms by Citroën enthusiasts around the world as the model that at last marks a return to the adventurous design values for which the French car-maker was long famous.

Although it is a well-priced hatchback that must compete for sales with the likes of the VW Golf, Opel Astra and Toyota Corolla, the C4 is quite strikingly different in both its profile and its detailing, ensuring that it stands out from the crowd. The radical approach begins with the novel interpretation of the Citroën logo, which echoes the design previously seen on both the C-Airdream and C-Airlounge concepts. The twin parallel chrome strips that make up the grille rise to form the famous chevron in the centre and extend outward into the boomerang-shaped lights that cut up into wings, this linking of chrome and glass visually widening the car.

There are two C4 models, a three-door coupé and a five-door saloon, both sharing their platform with the Peugeot 307. The main difference between their two sillhouettes is that the roof on the three-door extends rearward right over to the back bumper, creating a striking arched shape, whereas the five-door has been rounded off and is much less edgy.

The host of technical innovations includes swivelling xenon headlamps, laminated side windows, cruise control, and even a perfume dispenser on the dashboard. The central instrument display automatically adjusts in relation to the ambient light conditions to ensure a clear read-out. There is also a lane departure warning system, while a world first is the fixed-centre steering wheel, allowing optimally placed controls and the best possible shape for the driver's airbag.

The C4 shows the way forward with much more striking design language from Citroën and is to be warmly applauded.

Citroën C6

Engine	3.0 V6 (2.7 V6 diesel also offered)
Power	160 kW (215 bhp) @ 6000 rpm
Torque	290 Nm (214 lb. ft.) @ 3752 rpm
Gearbox	6-speed automatic
Installation	Front-engined/front-wheel drive
Front suspension	Double wishbone hydropneumatic
Rear suspension	Multi-link hydropneumatic
Brakes front/rear	Discs/discs
Length	4910 mm (193.3 in.)
Width	1860 mm (73.2 in.)
Height	1460 mm (57.5 in.)
Wheelbase	2900 mm (114.2 in.)

Citroën has taken a lot of criticism in recent years for cautious designs – something that the marque's fans believe represents a desertion of the futuristic values for which Citroën has long been celebrated.

However, such recent designs as the C3 and C4 have begun once again to show a more creative side to the brand. And now with the C6 Citroën at last returns to what many insist it does best: making big, luxurious and futuristic limousines to excite and inspire.

Long, elegant and charismatic, the C6 turns Citroën's double chevron logo into a distinctive full-width grille. The whole car sits close to the ground and is very streamlined; the long pointed bonnet leads to a fast A-pillar which in turn leads on to the roof that sweeps back in a continuous arc, gradually sloping down at the rear towards the boot.

The front and rear lamps have highly distinctive shapes from whatever angle they are viewed. From the side, the C6's sleekness is emphasized by the chrome strip that runs the length of the body, and the chrome trim outlining the windows. The waistline droops slightly at the rear, reminding the onlooker that the C6 is more about comfort and luxury than overt performance. At the rear, the overall form is rounded, the rear window concave.

The interior is less unconventional but nevertheless interesting, with its head-up display and sunken instrument panel in front of the driver and display screen in the centre. Imposing clusters of switches are to be found on the steering column and centre console.

Exciting and adventurous, the new C6 is unquestionably a worthy heir to the tradition of innovation inspired by the DS, the CX and the XM.

Dodge Caliber

Design	Trevor Creed
Front tyres	245/45R19
Rear tyres	245/45R19
Length	4414 mm (173.8 in.)
Width	1743 mm (68.6 in.)
Height	1534 mm (60.4 in.)
Wheelbase	2635 mm (103.7 in.)
Track front/rear	1520/1520 mm (59.8/59.8 in.)

To be bold, confident and assertive is the new mission of Dodge, say senior Chrysler Group strategists. The new Caliber, at present just another concept but due to enter full production in 2006, will be an important element in that strategy.

Dodge aims to be a volume brand, even in Europe, and the Caliber is one of its chosen weapons. If the warm reception given to the concept at the 2005 Geneva show is anything to go by, Dodge may have hit on a format that could click very successfully with the notoriously choosy European customer.

Success is something that eluded the Chrysler Neon, which the Caliber will replace. The Neon, a four-door sedan, is easy enough to define – but the Caliber is much harder to categorize. On one level it is a compact station-wagon the size of a Ford Focus, yet there are elements of an SUV's toughness, too – while the profile of the glasshouse is distinctly reminiscent of a coupé, despite the presence of four doors and a hatchback.

The whole design uses boldly carved features, starting at the front with Dodge's signature cross-hair grille, and a raised bonnet giving a hint of retro. The waist rail is high and rises towards the rear, with a sharp ledge created as it drops over on to the slab-sided door.

The design grabs attention from every angle: its rugged air is helped by bulging wheel arches with 19-inch wheels, although the low-profile tyres look out of place with such bold arch treatment. Black appliqué runs the length of the roof and draws in the spoiler, visually toning down the upper body. It is a clever design in the way it appears larger than it actually is, but whether Europeans will take to something so overtly masculine is another question.

Dodge Charger

Engine	5.7 V8 (3.5 V6 also offered)
Power	254 kW (340 bhp) @ 5000 rpm
Torque	525 Nm (387 lb. ft.) @ 4000 rpm
Gearbox	5-speed automatic
Installation	Front-engined/rear-wheel drive
Front suspension	Double wishbone
Rear suspension	Multi-link
Brakes front/rear	Discs/discs
Front tyres	215/65R17
Rear tyres	215/65R17
Length	5082 mm (200 in.)
Width	1891 mm (74.4 in.)
Height	1479 mm (58.2 in.)
Wheelbase	3048 mm (120 in.)
Track front/rear	1600/1604 mm (63/63.1 in.)
Kerb weight	1828 kg (4030 lb.)
Fuel consumption	10.7 l/100 km (22 US mpg)

Made famous during the 1970s in the television series *The Dukes of Hazzard*, the original Dodge Charger was outrageous in its looks and power – the supreme example of the classic American muscle-car genre. In reviving the illustrious nameplate for the 2006 model year, Dodge has come up with a fresh interpretation that also projects a powerful and coupé-like appearance. Yet, though many of the design cues are familiar, the proportions are very different and – to the surprise of many, some of whom accuse Dodge of having gone soft – four-door practicality now comes as standard.

As a percentage of the overall vehicle length the cabin has been extended to make space for the extra doors; Dodge has been clever in giving what is now a sedan the muscular feel of the old coupé Charger through the sharp kick-up in the horizontal waistline at the back of the rear doors as it meets the raised plane of the boot lid. The Charger's boot is cut short, again emphasizing the sporty aspirations of the model and, says parent company Chrysler, improving the aerodynamics. The fast rear screen is flanked by sculpted pillars, which once more hint at the flying buttress C-pillars of past Chargers.

The front end is bold, with a forward-leaning grille that gives the whole car a tilted-forward stance; the lamps in particular look menacing, the sharply angled tops of their housings partially cutting off the inner pair of lights and forming the leading edge of the front fenders. Inside, the cabin is routine rather than exciting.

The angry-looking image projected by the Charger may not win any design prizes but is sure to find a resonance with American muscle-car fans eager to relive the fast and furious days of their youth.

Dodge Nitro

Design	Trevor Creed
Engine	3.7 V6
Power	157 kW (210 bhp) @ 5200 rpm
Torque	319 Nm (235 lb. ft.) @ 4000 rpm
Gearbox	4-speed automatic
Installation	Front-engined/four-wheel drive
Front suspension	Short and long arm
Rear suspension	Five-link solid axle
Brakes front/rear	Discs/discs
Front tyres	255/50R20
Rear tyres	255/50R20
Length	4543 mm (178.9 in.)
Width	1857 mm (73.1 in.)
Height	1758 mm (69.2 in.)
Wheelbase	2752 mm (108.3 in.)
Kerb weight	1867 kg (4116 lb.)
0–100 km/h (62 mph)	9.6 sec
Top speed	174 km/h (108 mph)

Part of Dodge's 2005 concept vehicle assault is the mid-size Nitro SUV, designed to gain a presence in a market dominated by the Cherokee produced by its sister brand Jeep. Bold and powerful, the new Dodge is indeed based on Jeep hardware. The concept car on show at Chicago had a bright red exterior, making a clear statement about its high-energy personality.

At the front the Dodge cross-hair grille is as prominent as ever, with chrome bands leading out each side to rectangular headlamps. Notable are the very wide horizontal fenders, which join the raised bonnet almost in the manner of a truck or a prewar car.

The overall proportions of the bonnet-cabin section are boxy, with a high waistline that cocoons the occupants and seats them high up above the road. The body is made up of mainly rectangular elements that, together with some circular sections and the very taut surfaces, give it a contemporary twist. The C-pillar has been blacked out to help emphasize length, while the flat clamshell bonnet has opening lines that run rearward and then up and over the doors. Behind the front wheel arches are brushed-silver vents in the fashion of the latest Range Rover. Viewed from the rear, the Nitro majors on rectangular elements for a purposeful look.

The extensive satin-silver console inside the cabin looks stylish: Dodge should resist pressure to tone this down for a production model. The steering wheel, on the other hand, looks like an incongruous afterthought. Clever loading arrangements include a one-piece lift-up tailgate and a sliding cargo deck to ease the stowage of heavy items.

Tough and imposing in its stance, the Nitro may go down well in the USA but would have to be toned down for European tastes.

Dodge Ram Mega-Cab

Design	Rick Aneiros
Engine	5.7 V8 (5.9 in-line 6 diesel also offered)
Power	463 kW (345 bhp) @ 5400 rpm
Torque	509 Nm (375 lb. ft.) @ 4200 rpm
Gearbox	5-speed automatic
Installation	Front-engined/four-wheel drive
Front suspension	Live axle, four-link arms
Rear suspension	Live axle, leaf spring
Brakes front/rear	Discs/discs
Length	6292 mm (247.7 in.)
Width	2019 mm (79.5 in.)
Height	1994 mm (78.5 in.)
Wheelbase	4072 mm (160.3 in.)
Track front/rear	1765/1732 mm (69.5/68.2 in.)
Kerb weight	3015 kg (6647 lb.)

There could be no more appropriate name for the Mega-Cab. At about 6 metres (20 ft.) long, it is a monster and, according to Dodge, the biggest pickup in the world.

As with all Dodge trucks, the Mega-Cab's front end is dominated by the huge grille that communicates to the onlooker the vehicle's immense size and power. From the side the proportions are more informative: the long cabin clearly shows that interior space and comfort are of vital importance, a fact demonstrated by the designers having allowed the rear seats to recline. The rear bed is still able to carry the all-important 2.4 x 1.2 metre (8 x 4 ft.) boards with the tailgate down; so equal priority is given to comfort and functionality. There are huge gaps above the wheels for long articulation when off-roading with a heavy load.

Despite its size, there are just a few exterior treatment details, mainly because the Mega-Cab does not really need detailing in order to stand out. There are some longitudinal feature lines that run through the doors, and the waistline runs along the daylight opening line rearward on to the load-bay side, all of which lengthen the Mega-Cab and break up some of its height.

The interior has some high-spec features, including a roof-mounted DVD player for the rear seat passengers, and a mix of wood and leather trim. Despite this, the interior design lacks cohesiveness at the expense of focusing on function. The shapes that form the centre console, for example, look cluttered and without clear rationale.

91

Etud Intégral Scooto

Design	Etud Design
Engine	T-Max Yamaha
Gearbox	Sequential
Installation	Mid-engined/rear-wheel drive
Front suspension	Leading link
Rear suspension	Trailing link
Length	2400 mm (94.5 in.)
Width	1400 mm (55.1 in.)
Height	1400 mm (55.1 in.)
Wheelbase	1800 mm (70.9 in.)
Top speed	90 km/h (56 mph)
Fuel consumption	<3 l/100 km (>94.2 mpg)
CO₂ emissions	74 g/km

The Scooto concept is another clear example of why such companies as Etud Intégral will be the ones to push the boundaries in car design. This attractive and futuristic-looking idea for urban transport sits between the scooter and the Smart-size micro-urban vehicle: it aims to offer the main benefits of a traditional scooter in terms of open-air feel and manoeuvrability while also providing some of the practicalities of a car, such as basic weather protection and the ability to carry up to three people.

With compact dimensions – it is shorter than a Smart at 2.4 metres (7 ft. 10 in.), and only 1.4 metres (4 ft. 7 in.) wide – it is classified in the quad category, meaning that in some countries it can be driven at a younger age than for cars and with only a scooter licence. The package allows it to transport either two adults in tandem or one adult and two children. The design breaks with convention: the basis to the concept is a moulded floor structure with a large, pivoting curved windscreen that doubles as the roof when swung back in place. Like a scooter this is a very open vehicle with no doors, so it offers only a small amount of storage. The question of crash protection would also need to be addressed were this concept to be considered for production. Power, according to Etud, could be supplied by either a motorcycle engine or a gas or electric motor.

Similar concepts have been shown in the past, but a well-defined market would have to be demonstrated before a manufacturer would be prepared to get behind this idea. The much more carlike Smart has been a big success but BMW's C1 two-wheeler with a roof was a flop – so the potential for an affordable Scooto-type vehicle bridging the gap is hard to gauge.

Farboud GTS

Design	Arash Farboud
Engine	3.0 V6
Power	265 kW (355 bhp) @ 6200 rpm
Gearbox	6-speed manual
Installation	Mid-engined/rear-wheel drive
Front suspension	Double wishbone
Rear suspension	Double wishbone
Brakes front/rear	Discs/discs
Front tyres	245/35ZR19
Rear tyres	285/35ZR19
Length	4400 mm (173.2 in.)
Width	1850 mm (72.8 in.)
Height	1400 mm (55.1 in.)
Wheelbase	2675 mm (105.3 in.)
Kerb weight	1055 kg (2326 lb.)
0–100 km/h (62 mph)	3.9 sec

The Farboud GTS demonstrates the best in the long tradition of British entrepreneurial sports-car spirit. Arash Farboud, a man with a vision to create a unique roadgoing supercar inspired by Le Mans and GT cars, has brought together a team of experts to create a new road and race car.

The result is the very attractive GTS, which successfully conveys precisely those cues. All the well-established race-bred technologies are incorporated, such as a carbon-fibre chassis tub, a mid-engined mechanical layout and a powerful aerodynamic shape.

At the front the style is classic supercar, Ferrari meets McLaren F1 and Lotus Elise perhaps – the latter not so surprising as Farboud is based in Norfolk, England, home also to Lotus Cars. Large openings cut into the doors behind the front wheels allow escaping hot air from the front-mounted radiators to run freely out along the car's flanks.

The distinctive shoulder styling line that runs the length of the car drops over the rear wheel, allowing an original and attractive rear lamp treatment but lowering the visual weight and power at the rear wheels. At the rear the high exhausts and functional black venturi tunnels dominate. The interior is fitted out in aluminium, leather and carbon fibre, to provide a lightweight yet high-tech ambience.

For a car designed and built by a small team, the Farboud has achieved a credible style made up of some unique elements, even if the fundamental mid-engined supercar concept is a tried and tested one. The real challenge with any ambitious and well-meaning individual project such as this is the ramp-up to business profitability. To finance production, customer deposits are needed – and people with supercar money tend to want a credible brand, not a fragile start-up.

Fenomenon Stratos

Design	Fenomenon
Engine	V8
Power	312 kW (419 bhp) @ 8500 rpm
Torque	373 Nm (275 lb. ft.) @ 4750 rpm
Gearbox	6-speed manual
Installation	Mid-engined/rear-wheel drive
Front suspension	Double wishbone
Rear suspension	Double wishbone
Brakes front/rear	Discs/discs
Length	3932 mm (154.8 in.)
Width	1941 mm (76.4 in.)
Height	1251 mm (49.3 in.)
Wheelbase	2275 mm (89.6 in.)
Kerb weight	950 kg (2094 lb.)

Inspired by the Lancia Stratos and its famous rally successes during the 1970s, Christian Hrabalek, founder of Fenomenon, set about creating a modern Stratos. The new car, paradoxically, is conceived for developing countries without high-quality roads, but where there are pockets of wealthy people who might be inspired by a new and unique automotive supercar with iconic roots.

The body picks up on some of the original Stratos design cues such as the short wheelbase, the pointed front end and the wrapped, visor-like windscreen. Gone, however, are the pop-up headlamps, replaced by more modern alternatives. The waistline is raised and additional creases have been added to the body for a look that is more current than the much simpler 1970s shape.

The result is a car that is instantly identifiable as a Stratos, but with sharper detailing and an even more purposeful look.

Fenomenon is a new, holistic design agency based in London, and the Stratos project was the first to demonstrate the group's skills. Launching a concept car is a big achievement from a small company and we can expect to see more from Fenomenon in future. The Stratos concept car was made possible by a small group of shareholders, all with deep enthusiasm for the original Stratos, and with no involvement from the Fiat group.

There is not yet any indication of likely pricing should Hrabalek decide to go into limited production with the design. With the prototype having a Ferrari V8 engine aboard and a select group of customers likely to settle for only the finest materials, the cost is sure to be substantial. Fenomenon will be aware of competition from many other high-quality offerings, but few of them are such highly focused two-seaters – and none wears the legendary Stratos badge.

Ferrari F430

Design	Pininfarina
Engine	4.3 V8
Power	360 kW (483 bhp) @ 8500 rpm
Torque	465 Nm (343 lb. ft.) @ 5250 rpm
Gearbox	6-speed sequential manual
Installation	Mid-engined/rear-wheel drive
Front suspension	Double wishbone
Rear suspension	Double wishbone
Brakes front/rear	Discs/discs
Front tyres	225/35ZR19
Rear tyres	285/35ZR19
Length	4512 mm (177.6 in.)
Width	1923 mm (75.7 in.)
Height	1214 mm (47.8 in.)
Wheelbase	2600 mm (102.4 in.)
Track front/rear	1669/1616 mm (65.7/63.6 in.)
Kerb weight	1450 kg (3197 lb.)
0–100 km/h (62 mph)	4 sec
Top speed	>315 km/h (>196 mph)

A new Ferrari is always a big event for enthusiasts and designers alike, and the replacement for the highly successful 360 Modena has been especially eagerly anticipated. The F430 may share the bonnet, doors and roof of the outgoing model, but the overall look is surprisingly different.

The fresh impression is created mainly by the much larger twin air intakes that divide the lower portion of the nose, echoing the frontal treatment of the famous sports-racing Ferraris of the 1960s. The look is more powerful and muscular as a result, reflecting the substantially greater power of the new 4.3-litre powerplant. This gorgeously symmetrical engine, with its red crackle-finished airboxes, is deliberately displayed to admiring onlookers through the rear window, the perfect advertisement for Ferrari technology. At the very rear the influence of aerodynamics on the F430's design is clearly visible, with the large, two-channel air diffuser a prominent sculptural element, highlighted in black, its role being to provide all-important downforce for cornering at high speeds.

For Ferrari 2004 was an outstanding year in terms of Formula One success, with a sixth successive constructor's title and Michael Schumacher's fifth driver's title in a row. One of the innovations transferred from Formula One to the F430 is the E-diff electronic differential system, controlled by a 'manettino' rotary knob on the steering wheel. Its five modes, ranging from Race to Sport and even Ice, manage the systems governing vehicle dynamics for optimum driveability and stability. Also F1-derived are the paddle-operated sequential gearbox with shift times down to 150 milliseconds, the optional carbon-ceramic brakes, and the smooth underbody and diffuser aerodynamics.

The F430 is likely to be a big seller in Ferrari terms: almost two-thirds of Ferraris sold are eight-cylinder models, and it is replacing the most successful Ferrari ever made.

99

Fiat Croma

Design	Italdesign Giugiaro
Engine	2.4 in-line 4 diesel (1.8 and 2.2 petrol, and 1.9 diesel, also offered)
Power	149 kW (200 bhp) @ 4000 rpm
Torque	400 Nm (295 lb. ft.) @ 2000 rpm
Gearbox	6-speed automatic
Installation	Front-engined/front-wheel drive
Front suspension	MacPherson strut
Rear suspension	Multi-link
Brakes front/rear	Discs/discs
Front tyres	215/50R17
Rear tyres	225/45R18
Length	4750 mm (187 in.)
Width	1770 mm (69.7 in.)
Height	1600 mm (63 in.)
Wheelbase	2700 mm (106.3 in.)
Track front/rear	1513/1496 mm (59.6/58.9 in.)
Kerb weight	1650 kg (3638 lb.)
0–100 km/h (62 mph)	8.5 sec
Top speed	216 km/h (134 mph)
Fuel consumption	8 l/100 km (35 mpg)
CO_2 emissions	212 g/km

There is much that is puzzling about the Fiat Croma. Not least of the questions is why it exists at all.

Fiat has been in serious trouble on almost every front, and every euro spent on car development needs to be spent developing the right cars. The Croma is a large car, and Fiat has a poor track record in selling large cars: if such a respected volume car-maker as Renault can concede that its stylish and well-built Vel Satis luxury car has failed to hit the mark, what hope is there for an offering from Fiat, which has zero credibility among big-car buyers?

Given that Fiat wanted to develop a big car, the sharing of the platform with strategic partner General Motors' Opel Signum is a logical enough move. Yet the style chosen for that big car is another puzzle: though the lines were penned by the maestro, Giorgetto Giugiaro at Italdesign, the format of a large and bulky semi-estate, semi-hatchback is baffling. Hatchbacks have a notoriously bad time in the premium sectors, while estates have to project a sense of style and class in order to attract upmarket customers.

Uncharacteristically, Giugiaro's design fails to deliver on any of these qualities. The proportions are awkward, even if some of the detailing is pleasing: large headlamps and a plain rectangular chrome grille sit at the base of the steep bonnet that rises sharply, MPV-style, from a long overhang, breaking only slightly at the windscreen wipers before continuing up over a fast screen. The D-pillar leans forward and, in combination with the satin roof rails, lightens the overall look; the interior is well laid out and restrained in its materials and presentation.

Nevertheless, at a time when Fiat needs to be brilliant, the Croma is merely competent. Worse, it is the wrong car for Fiat.

Ford Explorer Sport Trac

Engine	4.6 V8
Installation	Front-engined/four-wheel drive
Front suspension	Short and long arm
Rear suspension	Trailing arm
Brakes front/rear	Discs/discs
Front tyres	P295/45R21
Rear tyres	P295/45R21
Length	5354 mm (210.8 in.)
Width	1897 mm (73.7 in.)
Height	1826 mm (71.9 in.)
Wheelbase	3315 mm (130.5 in.)
Track front/rear	1547/1575 mm (60.9/62 in.)

The first generation of Ford's sport utility truck was said to have invented the market sector when it was launched back in 2001. Although this latest Sport Trac offering is merely a concept, it is expected that the production version will be extremely similar to this. That production model will be especially significant for Ford as it will be the first of the new-generation Explorers. Traditionally, the Explorer has been Ford's bestselling product family and often the world's bestselling vehicle.

The overall style of the new Sport Trac has a very of-the-minute feel to it; single-coloured body panels stretch from roof to sill, with only a handful of details and no chrome to break up the large surfaces. A gap runs along the base of the doors and up the back of the cab to make the cabin appear to float above the chassis.

The blacked-out B-pillar and tight shut lines play a clever trick on the viewer, giving the appearance of one long door on each side rather than the two that are actually fitted. At the front the large mesh grilles are set back within milled aluminium surrounds to highlight the power from within the tall engine bay; air outlets are set into the trailing edge of the front fenders, again signifying speed and power.

Proportionally, the new sport utility truck looks strong and purposeful, with huge 21-inch wheels, red brake calipers and a lowered body. Inside, there is a contemporary feel with pale colours, simple shapes with chrome trimming, and a tall centre console housing the navigation system.

With the market for sport utility trucks continuing to grow, Ford needs to stay ahead of the competition to preserve its volumes and protect one of the biggest profit-earners in its US operations; this model could do the trick.

Ford Fairlane

Design	Kris Tommason
Engine	3.0 V6
Power	157 kW (210 bhp) @ 6250 rpm
Torque	271 Nm (200 lb. ft.) @ 4750 rpm
Gearbox	6-speed automatic
Installation	Front-engined/rear-wheel drive
Front suspension	MacPherson strut
Rear suspension	Multi-link
Brakes front/rear	Discs/discs
Front tyres	255/55R19
Rear tyres	255/55R19
Length	4834 mm (190.3 in.)
Width	1943 mm (76.5 in.)
Height	1717 mm (67.6 in.)
Wheelbase	2916 mm (114.8 in.)
Track front/rear	1674/1707 mm (65.9/67.2 in.)

Tall, boxy and upright, but with rounded corners and a curiously Range Rover-like relationship between its glasshouse and its flat bonnet, the Fairlane is a Ford concept that seeks to bring together the appeal of a station-wagon, a people-carrier and an SUV. Like so many Ford-group products, it is based on the front-wheel-drive architecture of the mid-size Mazda 6.

In its interior design, too, the Fairlane seeks to explore new ideas and concepts. The cabin is split into a driver-focused front row, a luxury second row and a more flexible third row that can be adapted to carry luggage if required. There is a glass roof that runs the length of the cabin and has separate sections to help emphasize the zones.

The driver zone has a particularly low and spacious dash that aids visibility but seems strangely at odds with the boxy exterior. A horizontal plywood panel runs across the dashboard and temporarily breaks and lifts over the instruments: this same finish is found on the door panels, where brushed-aluminium accents also feature on the window and door-lock controls.

The middle zone uses canvas on the seats, which give adult-size comfort and recline. The third zone has simpler seats, which, when folded, leave a practical stainless-steel load floor that is easily cleaned. The rear tailgate contains a novelty: a small refrigerator and food preparation area.

Externally the Fairlane looks sophisticated and dignified, thanks in part to its Land Rover-like 'floating' roof – though the parallel grooves running along the centre-opening doors count as an unnecessarily fussy detail in what is otherwise a strong and attractive design.

Ford Fairlane **Concept** 105

Ford Focus

Design	Claudio Messale
Engine	2.0 in-line 4 (1.4 and 1.6, and 1.6 and 2.0 diesel, also offered)
Power	107 kW (144 bhp) @ 6000 rpm
Torque	185 Nm (136 lb. ft.) @ 4500 rpm
Gearbox	5-speed manual
Installation	Front-engined/front-wheel drive
Front suspension	MacPherson strut
Rear suspension	Multi-link
Brakes front/rear	Discs/discs
Front tyres	205/55R16
Rear tyres	205/55R16
Length	4342 mm (170.9 in.)
Width	1991 mm (78.4 in.)
Height	1447 mm (57 in.)
Wheelbase	2640 mm (103.9 in.)
Kerb weight	1356 kg (2990 lb.)
0–100 km/h (62 mph)	9.2 sec
Top speed	206 km/h (128 mph)
Fuel consumption	7.1 l/100 km (39.8 mpg)
CO_2 emissions	170 g/km

The original Focus was a revelation when it replaced the long-serving Escort back in 1998. Razor-edged, contemporary and highly identifiable, the Focus has been a huge success – but what are we expected to think of its replacement?

Gone are some of the bullish design statements: the bonnet line is flatter than before, the headlamps make less of a visual impact and the larger grille, ringed in chrome, echoes that of the flagship Ford Five Hundred saloon from the USA.

Although less striking than before, the front is classically modern; the main area of surprise comes with the hatchback versions, where the slimness of the C-pillars is accentuated by the relatively large body panel below. If the rear screen had been more upright, with more visual weight to the car's upper architecture, the whole impression would have been more dynamic – surely a good thing, especially for the sportier three-door.

By comparison, the saloon's looks are much more successful. The more balanced profile provided by the extra visual mass of the boot makes for a classier overall impression, enhanced by a subtle straight crease running front to rear from the large wheel arch through the chunky door handles and into the rear lamp, and by the long upper glass area that extends into the rear pillar.

Inside, the interior has undergone a complete change, abandoning the old car's radical mix of intersecting arcs for a more conventional symmetrical instrument panel with air vents in the familiar Ford oval shape. The effect is more upmarket than youthful or sporty.

In terms of engineering there is no question that, like its forebear, the new Focus is dynamically superb, especially considering its keen price. In terms of design, however, Ford must take care not to let its Focus brand identity become diluted.

Ford Focus Vignale

Engine	2.0 in-line 4
Power	107 kW (145 bhp) @ 6000 rpm
Torque	185 Nm (136 lb. ft.) @ 4500 rpm
Gearbox	5-speed manual
Installation	Front-engined/front-wheel drive
Front suspension	MacPherson strut
Rear suspension	Multi-link
Brakes front/rear	Discs/discs
Width	1991 mm (78.4 in.)
Wheelbase	2640 mm (103.9 in.)

While the hatchback versions of the new Ford Focus met with a cool response from the design community when they were presented at the Paris show in 2004, the Focus Vignale concept that formed the highlight of the Ford display was much more enthusiastically received.

Named after designer Alfredo Vignale, whose Italian coachbuilding firm created sports cars for Ferrari, Maserati and Lancia in the 1950s and 1960s, the Vignale concept is in effect a convertible version of the Focus saloon, using the nowadays obligatory rigid retracting roof system.

Initially billed by Ford at the 2004 Paris show as a "one-off design study to explore the potential for future Focus derivatives", the Vignale soon demonstrated that potential, and it was little more than six weeks afterwards that Ford announced it was to put the Focus Vignale concept into production in 2006. Under this plan the vehicle will be developed and manufactured by Italy's Pininfarina, the same company that makes the Streetka.

There are clear similarities with the base Focus but the Vignale has some important differences that give it a larger, classier look. Width and length are emphasized by a new-look three-bar upper chrome grille, an egg-crate lower grille and aluminium detailing round the front air ducts and exhaust outlets, together with horizontal strips along the boot lid and side sills.

Blue-green tinted-glass panels dominate the retractable hard-top that stows away in the boot. Inside, the cabin is trimmed in plush leather and suede, with a two-tone facia panel and contrasting seat stitching and ribbing, giving it a very special and luxurious feel.

Compared with the bland standard Focus, the Vignale is a much more resolved design – and one that will appeal to the showy cabriolet set, too.

Ford Fusion

Design	J. Mays
Engine	3.0 V6 (2.3 in-line 4 also offered)
Power	156.6 kW (210 bhp) @ 6250 rpm
Torque	271 Nm (200 lb. ft.) @ 4750 rpm
Gearbox	6-speed automatic
Installation	Front-engined/front-wheel drive
Front suspension	Independent short and long arm
Rear suspension	Multi-link
Brakes front/rear	Discs/discs
Front tyres	205/60TR16
Rear tyres	205/60TR16
Length	4831 mm (190.2 in.)
Width	1834 mm (72.2 in.)
Height	1417 mm (55.8 in.)
Wheelbase	2728 mm (107.4 in.)
Track front/rear	1565/1557 mm (61.6 /61.3 in.)
Kerb weight	1488 kg (3280 lb.)

The inspiration for the Ford Fusion was seen two years ago in Ford's 427 concept, widely hailed as a rebirth of home-grown American design. Many of the 427's design features are carried forward into this production model – in particular the bold three-bar grille and the projector headlamps. The car as a whole, however, is smaller: like so many other Fords it is built on the international CD3 Mazda 6 platform, though its allotted task in the US market is to replace the bulky and unloved Ford Taurus.

The Fusion is specifically conceived as a classic American mid-size saloon that, although not expensive in relation to its competitors, is imbued with a higher perceived value thanks to its long proportions, wide C-pillar and short boot lid, all of which serve to emphasize solidity and integrity.

When the car is viewed from the front, the eye is drawn both outward to the large headlamps and inward to the thrust-forward grille and its central Ford logo; also noticeable is the grounded stance created by what is termed 'tumblehome', the amount the doors angle in towards the roof.

Along the side runs a subtle feature line parallel to the rising waistline. This measured rise makes the rear door glass shallower than that at the front, but the roof surface is kept parallel to the ground so that headroom for rear seat passengers is not compromised.

Inside, one of the three grades of fabric available is white-stitched charcoal-black leather. This smart combination again lends itself to an impression of quality. The interior design of the Fusion shows a clear European influence and is a marked improvement over many past Fords. Coupled with a strong exterior design that has been carefully honed for proportion and detail, a convincing new package is the result.

Ford SAV

Ford is embarking on a new phase of design inspiration and openly states that the new SAV, displayed at the 2005 Geneva show, gives a strong insight into the future design direction the company's European strategists intend to adopt.

It is easy to see why Ford is so eager to advertise its latest design thinking. The SAV is about the same size as the current Galaxy, but that is where the similarity ends. Visually dynamic and tightly packed, the SAV has flared wheel arches tightly filled with substantial wheels, while sharp lines run rearward from vents behind each front wheel arch. The front and rear lower bumpers have matt white trim panels that stylishly finish off the area; on the show concept the front trim was in orange – which lent the vehicle a racier, less subtle image.

The windscreen rises at a fast angle directly rearward from the bonnet, making a clear statement about this car as a monovolume with a clean shape. At the rear of the arched roof there is an integrated spoiler that partially umbrellas the rear screen. The side window shaping is strong, with the fixed quarter-window kicking up at the rear; the complete glass area is surrounded by a chrome band, again emphasizing its dynamic profile.

The interior, too, breaks new ground for Ford. It is fresh, clean and open, with an orange pinstripe featuring throughout. Orange detailing is repeated on the centre console, the instrument needles and the five seats, the rear three being electrically reconfigurable from a standard 2+3 combination to a more spacious 2+2+1, with the centre chair powering rearward to sit between the fitted luggage trolleys.

Here is promise, indeed, that the new design direction under Martin Smith will provide Ford with the trend-setting products it so badly needs.

Engine	In-line 4
Gearbox	6-speed manual
Installation	Front-engined/front-wheel drive
Front suspension	MacPherson strut
Rear suspension	Multi-link
Brakes front/rear	Discs/discs

Ford Shelby GR-1

Design	George Saridakis
Engine	6.4 V10
Power	451 kW (605 bhp) @ 6750 rpm
Torque	680 Nm (501 lb. ft.) @ 5550 rpm
Gearbox	6-speed manual
Installation	Front-engined/rear-wheel drive
Front suspension	Short and long arm
Rear suspension	Short and long arm
Brakes front/rear	Discs/discs
Front tyres	275/40R19
Rear tyres	345/35R19
Length	4412 mm (173.7 in.)
Width	1895 mm (74.6 in.)
Height	1168 mm (46 in.)
Wheelbase	2540 mm (100 in.)
Track front/rear	1600/1557 mm (63/61.3 in.)
Kerb weight	1770 kg (3900 lb.)

Resplendent in its polished aluminium bodywork, the Shelby Cobra concept is based on the platform of the 2004 Shelby concept, itself an open-topped tribute to the 1960s original. This new concept mimics the look of the Cobra coupés that competed in long-distance events – including the Le Mans 24 Hours.

As the metallic surface of the Shelby GR-1 acts like a dull mirror, the more detailed forms are difficult to see. Luckily the overall stance and shape are so dramatic that the impression is unmistakable: this is a racing-inspired design, with distinctive proportions built around the driver and the mechanical layout.

A long bonnet wraps the engine and dips forward to greet the cavernous, shark-like air intake at the very front: the design makes it easy to visualize how the cooling air passes through the radiators and then out through the bonnet louvres and up and over the windscreen. The headlamps are faired smoothly into wheel arches that first rise up over the wheel centre and then gently descend as they move rearward along the waist rail.

Massive visual power is focused at the rear wheels, with arches that sweep over and blend into the huge C-pillar and the sharp cut-off of the very high Kamm tail, an effect that creates a teardrop cabin and a narrow rear screen.

Inside, slate-grey Alcántara suede dominates the dashboard, the trim on the bucket seats and the rim of the flat-based steering wheel. Yet the porthole-style display screen in the centre of the dash sits uncomfortably with the highly focused, sporting exterior – as do innovations such as the noise-reducing speaker system and the blue-glow ambient cabin lighting. However, the tyres are equipped with sensors that transmit temperatures, pressures and cornering G-forces, and other racing touches include a starter button located in the top of the gear knob.

Ford SYNus

Design	José Paris
Engine	2.0 in-line 4 diesel
Power	100 kW (134 bhp)
Torque	320 Nm (236 lb. ft.)
Gearbox	5-speed manual
Installation	Front-engined/front-wheel drive
Front suspension	MacPherson strut
Rear suspension	Semi-independent torsion beam
Brakes front/rear	Discs/drums
Front tyres	225/50R18
Rear tyres	225/50R18
Length	4013 mm (158 in.)
Width	1760 mm (69.3 in.)
Wheelbase	2543 mm (100.1 in.)
Track front/rear	1529/1529 mm (60.2/60.2 in.)

As a vehicle providing a highly protective environment for urban travel, it may be questioned whether the SYNus is an idea that should be encouraged in today's confrontational and often paranoid society.

Based on a rather ordinary Ford Fiesta platform, the SYNus gives the impression of a bank safe on wheels. As such, it seeks to offer occupant protection on an unprecedented level – a mini armoured car that comes with a secure mode that activates protective shutters to cover the windscreen and side glass when attacked. There is no glass to the rear; the small recessed windows on each side are non-opening and bullet-resistant, and give the impression of impenetrability. The rear door looks as if it is made from solid steel and comes with a bank-vault-type coded rotary release wheel, while the driver's door is opened via a safe-style combination lock mounted to the B-pillar.

The proportion is wide, boxy and slab-sided, with a depressed roofline. At the front the headlamps are recessed into the high bonnet that leads to an upright and flat windscreen, while at the rear ultra-slim tail lights and CHMSL (centre high-mounted stop-light) are squeezed between the rear door and body. Mounted inside the rear door is the largest flat-screen LCD (45 in.) ever fitted to a vehicle, which can be used to monitor the outside world via the body-mounted rear-view cameras, to surf the internet or to play DVDs. The seating inside can be reconfigured to switch from forward-facing for travel to rear-facing for wide-screen entertainment.

Despite the cosmetic façade of security, one cannot help but wonder whether hardcore urban gangs would simply regard the SYNus as a challenge and promptly turn it on its side to enter with less difficulty from underneath. However, Ford's designers are not too worried, as the model will never be produced.

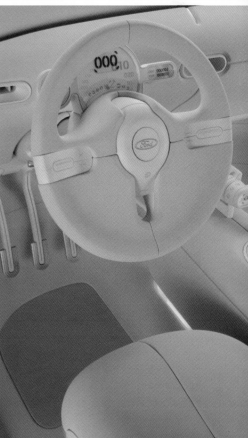

GM Sequel

Design	Robert Boniface
Engine	Hydrogen fuel cell
Power	73 kW (98 bhp)
Installation	Mid-mounted fuel cell/all-wheel drive
Length	4994 mm (196.6 in.)
Width	1966 mm (77.4 in.)
Height	1697 mm (66.8 in.)
Wheelbase	3040 mm (119.7 in.)
Kerb weight	2170 kg (4784 lb.)
0–100 km/h (62 mph)	10 sec
Top speed	145 km/h (90 mph)

As the world's number one auto-maker General Motors has only recently woken up to the need for vehicles friendly to the environment. One of its major commitments is to zero-emission hydrogen power: in 2002 and 2003 respectively it presented the Autonomy and Hy-wire concepts to demonstrate the packaging possibilities for this new type of propulsion.

The 2005 Sequel concept takes the fuel-cell strategy a major step further and is accompanied by a typically grand declaration from GM – that the reinvention of the automobile is no longer just a dream. In support of this assertion, GM claims that the Sequel has double the performance and twice the range of its predecessors, and that this visibly closer-to-production model, though still costly, uses already available technology and is notably less expensive to make.

In structural design terms the Sequel houses its three hydrogen cylinders and the fuel-cell block centrally under the passengers' feet; the lithium-ion battery sits between the rear wheels. Hub motors drive the rear wheels, a single central 73 kW unit powering the fronts.

The slender chassis gives the designers unusual freedom. The aesthetic design concept is all about interlocking elements that visually tighten the exterior and interior. Unfortunately, features relating to the fuel-cell power bring both stylistic and technical challenges. The cooling of the fuel-cell stack and motors is a primary concern: the Sequel's front end needs three large grille openings to draw in enough air. Still more air inlets can be found at the rear of the vehicle, below the lamps: these cool the rear wheel motors. LED lighting is used throughout as it uses less power and creates less heat.

GM stresses that this is no dream machine. Unconstrained by conventional architectures, the firm's designers must be relishing the opportunity to create truly inspirational products.

GMC Graphyte

While the primary mission of GMC's Graphyte concept is to provide visual proof of General Motors' conversion to the environmental cause – twelve hybrid models are promised over the next few years – it has an important secondary role as the ambassador for the new style language in which GM will present its new-wave, eco-friendly ranges.

The Graphyte still has the format of a large and imposing four-wheel-drive SUV and, at 5.3 litres and 300 bhp, its V8 engine is hardly modest. Yet, thanks to electric motors concealed within the transmission casing and a battery under the rear seat, GM is able to claim a 25% fuel saving over conventional petrol propulsion. The so-called two-mode hybrid system, co-developed with DaimlerChrysler, allows the Graphyte to mix petrol and electric power for optimum efficiency according to the driving conditions; in addition, the petrol engine can shut down two or four of its eight cylinders, depending on the power required.

The Graphyte's aesthetic design is the work of Simon Cox at GM's advanced studio in Coventry, England, and presents a subtly new take on the conventional set of SUV cues. A smooth front has the grille and headlamps angled back slightly, contrasting with the polished-metal H-shaped grille frame and lower rock shield. The windscreen is steeply raked, and the rear of the cabin is marked by distinctively triangular D-pillars, framing the high-mounted rear lights.

The rear is the most distinctive aspect of all, the underbody of the short overhang being cut away steeply to reveal another polished skidplate. A wide but shallow rear window gives the whole vehicle a broader, less intimidating look and helps it appear firmly planted on the road. Inside, apart from a central monitor displaying the hybrid system's status, it is more orthodox in its architecture.

Design	Simon Cox
Engine	5.3 V8 and two-motor electric hybrid
Power	224 kW (300 bhp) (petrol)
Torque	441 Nm (325 lb. ft.) (petrol)
Gearbox	4-speed automatic
Installation	Front-engined/all-wheel drive
Brakes front/rear	Discs/discs
Length	4768 mm (187.7 in.)
Width	2004 mm (78.9 in.)
Wheelbase	2895 mm (114 in.)

Honda Civic

At first glance you could be forgiven for thinking that the Civic concept was a coupé – it has a dramatically cab-forward stance, and the smooth sweep of its bonnet is carried almost uninterrupted up over the windscreen, along the roof and down the equally smooth tail. The car looks sleek, sporty and futuristically exciting.

Yet this is no racy two-plus-two but a five-door hatchback: developed for the European market, it is in fact the ambassador for the new, eighth-generation Civic, to be built at Honda's European manufacturing plant in Swindon, UK, from early 2006.

Honda readily admits that the concept is very close in its shape and much of its detailing to the eventual production model. As such, it marks a radical change of direction from the functional route chosen for the current model, which concentrates on space and practicality at the expense of style. Dowdiness is replaced with what looks very much like glamour, a premium style that radically repositions the Civic brand in relation to competitors that include the VW Golf and the Opel/Vauxhall Astra.

The impact of the Civic's striking shape is enhanced by innovative detailing. Headlamps and tail lamps are carried in distinctive glazed covers that span the full width of the car, creating a very prominent horizontal band at each end; at the back this sits below a ridge in the domed, darkened rear window that acts as an aerodynamic spoiler. On the side, a crease drawn rearward from the outer apex of the headlight takes in the single door handle and then meets the top of the rear light band. Enhancing the coupé look is the fact that the five-door version sees the rear door handle positioned above the waistline.

Alfa Romeo does just the same – so if Honda's aim was to put a touch of premium class into the new-generation Civic, it has certainly succeeded.

Engine	2.2 in-line 4 diesel (petrol also available)
Power	104 kW (140 bhp) @ 4000 rpm
Torque	340 Nm (250 lb. ft.) @ 2000 rpm
Gearbox	6-speed manual
Installation	Front-engined/front-wheel drive
Brakes front/rear	Discs/discs

Honda Civic Si

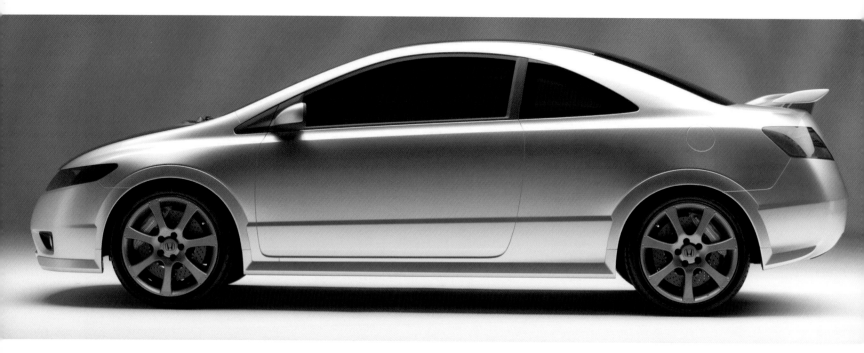

Power	149 kW (200 bhp)
Gearbox	6-speed manual
Installation	Front-engined/front-wheel drive
Brakes front/rear	Discs/discs
Front tyres	225/40R18
Rear tyres	225/40R18

The Civic Si coupé, presented at the 2005 Chicago show, previews the sixth-generation coupé variant of the forthcoming Civic range; it will be unique to North America and will debut late that same year.

The silhouette is distinctive, with a cab-forward stance, a proportion favoured by many of the world's fastest mid-engined cars. The A-pillars sweep forward at a very fast angle, joining the waistline over the front wheel; the short front end makes the compact packaging of Honda's V-TEC engine clearly evident.

The roof arches right to the back of the car, emphasizing the vehicle's sporty stance and improving cabin volume. A simple rising feature line runs through the doors to break up the body height. A narrow stepped finisher runs along the sills and up and over the wheel arches, grounding the Civic and maintaining its lightweight and nimble look.

The bonnet is finished in black to give visual continuity with the windscreen and roof, while at the rear Honda has specified a suspended wing to counteract the lift that is generated underneath the body of any car at high speed. The central exhaust is a neat feature of the concept but would be too expensive to include on the volume production version and is likely to be dropped.

Aimed primarily at the US market (where it will be manufactured, too) the production version of the Civic Si concept is still relatively conservative in its shaping, largely to suit the more cautious transatlantic tastes. It certainly lacks the radical streak of the Civic hatchback concept shown a few weeks later at the Geneva show – but it is nevertheless a welcome sign that a major car-maker is prepared to invest in a wide variety of body configurations to suit important regional preferences.

Honda FR-V

Engine	2.0 in-line 4 (1.7, and 2.2 diesel, also offered)
Power	110 kW (148 bhp) @ 6500 rpm
Torque	192 Nm (142 lb. ft.) @ 4000 rpm
Gearbox	6-speed manual
Installation	Front-engined/front-wheel drive
Front suspension	MacPherson strut
Rear suspension	Double wishbone
Brakes front/rear	Discs/discs
Front tyres	205/55R16
Rear tyres	205/55R16
Length	4285 mm (168.7 in.)
Width	1810 mm (71.3 in.)
Height	1610 mm (63.4 in.)
Wheelbase	2680 mm (105.5 in.)
Track front/rear	1550/1560 mm (61/61.4 in.)
Kerb weight	1470 kg (3241 lb.)
0–100 km/h (62 mph)	10.5 sec
Top speed	195 km/h (121 mph)
Fuel consumption	8.4 l/100 km (33.6 mpg)
CO_2 emissions	199 g/km

Some of the leading lights in Europe's booming medium MPV segment are now into their second-generation models, but Japan's Honda has left it until now to make its bid for a slice of this growing business. Buyers in this sector are principally aged over 35 and with children, a group that tends to be looking for practical features such as multi-configurable seating and storage, with style frequently a secondary consideration.

Often original in its approach, Honda has decided to go for both style and utility with its FR-V. Echoing the Fiat Multipla, it carries six people in two rows of three, with all seats independent to allow numerous possibilities in terms of passenger and luggage-carrying configurations. And with what can sometimes be a rather dull vehicle type, Honda has given the FR-V a distinctive look by making a strong feature of the large swept headlamps and bold chrome grille.

Viewed from the side, the profile is carlike, with a short bonnet and a steeply rising waistline; below the waist it has a feature line that runs from the front wheel arch back to split the rear lamp lenses. The spearhead design cue is used throughout: on the front bonnet, in front of the door mirrors, on the rear side window, rear door shut line and rear lamp; all these draw the eye towards the rear hatch of the FR-V which, with its angled backlight, is unique in its design. The large area of body panels helps to make the car look more spacious and protective of its occupants.

Inside, the dashboard curves outward towards the centre, finishing in an aluminium panel that contains the gearlever, climate controls and other functions. Comprehensive and complex, this design visually widens the car but fails to give the air of restfulness that one would perhaps expect.

Honda Ridgeline

Engine	3.5 V6
Power	190 kW (255 bhp) @ 5750 rpm
Torque	342 Nm (252 lb. ft.) @ 4500 rpm
Gearbox	5-speed automatic
Installation	Front-engined/four-wheel drive
Front suspension	MacPherson strut
Rear suspension	Multi-link
Brakes front/rear	Discs/discs
Front tyres	245/65R17
Rear tyres	245/65R17
Length	5253 mm (206.8 in.)
Width	1976 mm (77.8 in.)
Height	1786 mm (70.3 in.)
Wheelbase	3099 mm (122 in.)
Track front/rear	1704/1699 mm (67.1/66.9 in.)
Kerb weight	2065 kg (4552 lb.)
Fuel consumption	14.9 l/100 km (19 mpg)

In 2004 Honda signalled its intention to enter the US sport utility truck market with its well-received SUT concept. The 2005 production version, christened Ridgeline, follows that 2004 template almost to the millimetre, with the significant differences apparent only inside the five-seater double cab.

The Ridgeline is notable not only as Honda's first foray into the true heartland of the American automotive way of life – the heavy pickup truck – but also as a truck that successfully manages to combine some flair in its design and detailing with the rugged, muscular and durable look buyers prefer. The triangulated load bay in particular conveys strength, as do the square wheel arches and the heavy framing to the doors. From the front the relative smallness of the headlamp/turn signal units emphasizes the massiveness of the rest of the structure, a trick repeated either side of the broad tailgate with slender rear lights. Large cutouts in the wheel arch blisters advertise the traction and ground clearance offered by the chunky tyres, and the bumpers are more pronounced than on the concept version.

It is the interior that has seen the biggest changes over Honda's original SUT concept. Gone are the cold aluminium rails on the dashboard, now replaced by a softer and more conventional look, with darker plastics; the large single circular instrument makes way for a more familiar array of separate dials ranged in front of the driver.

It may be the ambassador for a new breed of sport utility trucks that combine functionality with style, but the Honda Ridgeline nevertheless makes little compromise on the heavy-duty practicality so important to Americans. It still offers a half-tonne payload and a two-and-a-half-tonne towing capability, and can accommodate a quad or two trailbikes on its cargo bed. Its success seems assured.

Hummer H3

Engine	3.5 in-line 5
Power	164 kW (220 bhp) @ 5600 rpm
Torque	305 Nm (225 lb. ft.) @ 2800 rpm
Gearbox	5-speed manual
Installation	Front-engined/four-wheel drive
Front suspension	Short and long arm
Rear suspension	Leaf spring live axle
Brakes front/rear	Discs/discs
Front tyres	265/75R16
Rear tyres	265/75R16
Length	4742 mm (186.7 in.)
Width	2170 mm (85.4 in.)
Height	1893 mm (74.5 in.)
Wheelbase	2842 mm (111.9 in.)
Track front/rear	1651/1664 mm (65/65.6 in.)
Kerb weight	2130 kg (4696 lb.)
0–100 km/h (62 mph)	<10 sec
Top speed	180 km/h (112 mph)
Fuel consumption	13 l/100 km (18 US mpg)

As the third major vehicle inspired by the Humvee, the Hummer H3 is a world apart from that legendary military original. First came the H1, in effect a civilianized version of the army vehicle; next was the H2, slightly less massive and considerably more civilized. Now comes the H3, again reduced in its proportions but no less imposing in its ruggedness or intimidation factor.

H1s were bought by Hollywood stars and H2s find their clientele among the merely very wealthy; the H3 is aimed at a wider – though inevitably still rarefied – audience.

As such there are new, less exaggerated dimensions. Compared with the H2, the H3 is 430 mm (17 in.) shorter and a vital 165 mm (6 in.) narrower – though it still measures 1900 mm (75 in.) across the body, or 2170 mm (85 in.) if the mirrors are included. A smaller vehicle means less weight and therefore a smaller, five-cylinder 3.5-litre engine and the promise of reduced fuel thirst: for the European market a diesel will be offered.

Despite the vehicle's smaller stature, Hummer claims the H3 can power through 40 cm (16 in.) of water at 30 km/h (20 mph) or 60 cm (23 in.) at 8 km/h (5 mph); it can climb 40cm (16in.) vertical steps and rocks, make its way through deep sand and race over sandy surfaces. Impressive stuff.

Unsurprisingly, the absolutely unique style of the Hummer brand is faithfully encapsulated in the H3. The wide track, short overhangs, huge tyres and massive ground clearance shine out a mile, as do the upright, rectangular windows and signature seven-slot louvred grille. At the back the swing rear door is now also used to mount the spare wheel – a first for Hummer as it improves interior space.

Comfort and refinement, remarkably, make their first appearance on a Hummer, with heated leather seats, an electric sliding sunroof and DVD navigation in evidence. But rest assured: the H3 still looks mighty tough on the outside.

Hyundai Portico

Engine	Petrol-electric hybrid
Gearbox	6-speed automatic
Installation	Front-engined with front and rear motors/ all-wheel drive
Brakes front/rear	Discs/discs
Front tyres	255/60R18
Rear tyres	255/60R18
Length	5000 mm (196.9 in.)
Width	2000 mm (78.7 in.)
Wheelbase	3070 mm (120.9 in.)

Dramatic in its appearance, especially with its counter-opening side doors wide open to display its lounge-like six-seat interior, the Portico concept is Hyundai's take on the modern, mid-market minivan. Like Fiat's Multipla and Honda's FR-V before it, the Portico chooses to arrange its seating in two rows of three, giving more space in the rear for luggage.

The concept also has a role as a demonstrator for the advanced technology that Hyundai is developing: its hybrid drive system links a V6 petrol engine to two electric motors – a 136 bhp (101 kW) unit driving the front wheels and an 83 bhp (62 kW) device for the rear axle, neatly providing all-wheel-drive capability.

Designed and built by Hyundai's Advanced Design Team in South Korea, the Portico employs classically curvaceous forms that collide into features like the fault lines between tectonic plates. The front of the bonnet has a sinewy ridge that sweeps back to the A-pillars, the grille featuring organic, leaflike vents that contrast strongly with the much more engineered-looking headlamps.

From the side the proportion is rearward-biased, with the emphasis on the cabin – a deliberate message that is reinforced by the line circumnavigating the design's unique door opening line. The twin side doors open from the centre outward to give wide, welcoming access to the interior, completely free of obstruction by any pillars; inside the cabin the colour scheme is vibrant and the design modern and appealing. Up top is a panoramic glass roof that can be darkened in strong sunlight.

As a concept the Hyundai Portico is at the same time striking and interesting. Its presentation is provocative and full of creative tension – something that is sure to be taken on board by the design community, but that might be slightly too uncomfortable for the mass market.

Hyundai Sonata

Hyundai has been quietly picking up sales at almost every level of the volume car market, and the new Sonata saloon is the Korean car-maker's latest bid for a share of the action in the upper medium segment, a sector dominated – in Europe, at least – by the VW Passat, BMW 3 Series and Audi A4.

The new design is a classic three-box shape and comes across as a conservative and somewhat bland offering that will never stand out from the crowd. Viewed from the front, the proportion is balanced, with each feature given equal priority in terms of space. This results in a generic look that is a sure guarantee of anonymity – yet as any designer would immediately realize, a brand seeking conquest sales would be well advised to cultivate a stronger frontal identity than this.

Running along the side at waist level is an angled shoulder that catches the light from above, giving the car a solidity that Hyundai cars have previously lacked. Overall, there is a lightweight and somewhat feminine feel, with large wheel-arch-to-tyre gaps, a small sill panel below the door and a general absence of features that might emphasize power or speed. At the rear, however, the lamp design works well, with horizontal bands of colour rising gradually to the outboard edge, echoing the profile of the headlamps.

The interior is clearly laid out and well specified. The two-tone dashboard adds interest but in fact a single colour or a closer colour balance would have made for a more restful and sophisticated cabin. A very safe and inoffensive design, the Sonata will appeal to many people owing to its keen price and classic looks. Reliability and quality will win the hearts of many, but visual excitement is not on the menu.

Infiniti Kuraza

There is a definite shock value to the Infiniti Kuraza concept: not only is it very large, with its wheels a massive 23 inches in diameter, but it has six doors and a baffling kink in its long, white roofline.

The Kuraza aims to be a large SUV that at the same time seeks to convey each of its six occupants in perfect luxury. This means that the third-row seats should be no less comfortable than the second row, something that space and cost considerations inevitably rule out in standard designs. Thus each passenger has his or her own door and, so that the third-row passengers do not feel second-class at the back of the Kuraza, the roof and third-row seats are raised so that they can get a panoramic view of the road ahead. Hence the kinked waist and roof.

Infiniti is Nissan's luxury brand, and for the Kuraza Nissan Design has shifted the focus from mere transportation to hospitality. The Kuraza would not be the primary vehicle in a family but one to be used for special occasions, reason the designers: for this motive they have not filled it with the gadgets we have come to expect in our everyday cars but have instead specified a long console running between the seats.

Japanese inspiration is seen in the design of such details as the shape of each seat back, said to be drawn from a layered kimono. The interior is beautiful, combining wood, leathers and silk; the spacious floating dashboard has wrap-around areas that sweep round the front occupants.

But while the exquisite interior shows how Japan can lead the world, the exterior has way too much visual energy for a car that is supposed to provide luxury and sophistication.

Design	Kojii Nagano
Front tyres	305/45R23
Rear tyres	305/45R23

Infiniti M

Design	Tsunehiro Kunimoto, Michinari Chiba
Engine	4.5 V8 (3.5 V6 also offered)
Power	250 kW (335 bhp) @ 6400 rpm
Torque	461 Nm (340 lb. ft.) @ 4000 rpm
Gearbox	5-speed automatic
Installation	Front-engined/rear-wheel drive
Front suspension	Double wishbone
Rear suspension	Multi-link
Brakes front/rear	Discs/discs
Front tyres	245/45R18
Rear tyres	245/45R18
Length	4892 mm (192.6 in.)
Width	1798 mm (70.8 in.)
Height	1509 mm (59.4 in.)
Wheelbase	2901 mm (114.2 in.)
Kerb weight	1791 kg (3948 lb.)
Fuel consumption	11.8 l/100 km (20 US mpg)

Infiniti's replacement for its M-series medium-large luxury car is based on the Nissan Fuga concept first shown at the Tokyo show in 2003. As such, it is a much more sophisticated design than the current model, yet retains enough Infiniti feel to ensure continuity of identity – an essential prerequisite in the image-conscious market for premium luxury cars.

As evidenced by this car, the new Infiniti style is much bolder than preceding designs, with the distinctive L-shaped headlamps drawn up into the bonnet and flowing rearward to form creases in the top of the front wing line; the side window profile is strongly arched, feeding into a large, sloping rear screen that gives more interior space, itself emphasized by the addition of the small sixth-light side windows. Moving to the rear, the lamps now feature LED technology and the boot lip is higher, giving more boot volume and a much more modern look. These changes in proportions, together with the generally more flowing body surfaces, are all signifiers of an upmarket model.

Inside there is much leather and aluminium trim, and selected exterior design themes are reprised in the dramatic sweep of the dashboard's architecture. A central control knob allows the driver to select the most important vehicle functions, such as navigation, audio and air-conditioning, in an easy and intuitive manner, just as on the smaller Nissan Primera. The Infiniti M is particularly notable for North America's first use of a lane departure warning system.

Infiniti is now becoming a much more recognized brand across the USA and will enter other regions in the next few years. This new luxury saloon, with a distinctive style that sets it apart from such competitors as Lexus and Cadillac, can only continue to raise the brand's identity.

Italdesign Mitsubishi Nessie

Design	Italdesign
Engine	Hydrogen-fuelled V8
Gearbox	Automatic
Installation	Front-engined/all-wheel drive
Brakes front/rear	Discs/discs
Front tyres	305/40R23
Rear tyres	305/40R23
Length	4600 mm (181 in.)
Width	1950 mm (76.8 in.)
Height	1810 mm (71.3 in.)
Wheelbase	2780 mm (109.4 in.)
Track front/rear	1650/1650 mm (65/65 in.)

According to Italdesign, who came up with the concept in collaboration with Mitsubishi and the German Linde Group, the Nessie is the answer to the issue of the day – the SUV.

From the Nessie's specification, which includes a hydrogen-fuelled V8 engine, it is clear that Italdesign believes that environmental compatibility is one of the issues the SUV must address. But from the presentation of the massive and oddly proportioned concept at the 2005 Geneva Motor Show, it is arguable whether the designers have been successful in their other mission, the wish to provide a friendlier public image for the SUV.

Italdesign claims that the Nessie is the first of an all-new configuration of vehicle, which it labels the '2.5 volume SUV Coupé' – indicating perhaps a halfway-house between a three-box saloon and a two-box hatchback.

The Nessie certainly looks different, standing intimidatingly high on its vast 23-inch wheels; this height makes it look too short and narrow, though it actually measures 4.6 metres (15 ft.) long and almost two metres (6 ft. 6 in.) wide. The effect is that of a grossly swollen child's toy.

The wheel arches form huge deep shields over the large wheels; the doors are inset and protected by the bright lower step, and carry transparent panels to aid in-town manoeuvres. Fussy detailing such as the superficial wheel arch screws and complex front and rear lights does nothing for the continuity of an already busy design.

The chunky lower body is contrasted by a slim cant rail that runs back under the aluminium roof cross-rail, complete with a V-shaped frame designed to convey sportiness. To allow easier access to the rear seats, there is a short rear door on the right-hand side only.

As a design exercise the Nessie is bold and powerful, yet ultimately unappealing: its purpose appears as oddball as its proportions.

Jaguar Advanced Lightweight Coupé

In the whole of this book there is no better example of precision surfaces and proportion than this car. Jaguar's Advanced Lightweight Coupé – the name gives a strong clue to the look of the 2006 XK8 – has no superfluous detailing: the admirer has simply to look and appreciate the beautiful shapes and forms for what they are.

From the front, the oval grille is clearly E-Type inspired, and eyelike headlamps lead into a long bonnet. The slim form then stretches back over the huge 21-inch wheels, with the powerful haunches over the rear wheel arches emphasizing that this is a refined high-performance machine. The surfaces are drawn taut over the mechanicals to keep the body slim and low, proclaiming this a finely honed thoroughbred that will cut through the air with minimal interference.

The original E-Type was an immensely powerful car for its day, yet it was visually slender and muscular at the same time. This is precisely what Ian Callum has succeeded in achieving in a much more modern context in the Advanced Lightweight Coupé.

From the rear three-quarter view the elegant chrome trim that runs round the side windows makes a poignant contrast to the shape of the rear lamps, whose outboard edges point sharply towards each side's rear wheel. The aluminium gills in front of the doors emphasize the power exuding from the engine bay; visually these break the flow of the lower architecture, but the broad, taut poise of a cat about to pounce is still abundantly clear.

The interior of the car is trimmed throughout in tan leather, with switches and panels in technically finished polished aluminium. It is just as classy as the exterior, underlining how important the Advanced Lightweight Coupé will be in providing an exciting template for the many new Jaguars to emerge over the coming years.

Design	Ian Callum
Engine	V8
Installation	Front-engined/rear-wheel drive
Brakes front/rear	Discs/discs
Front tyres	21 in.
Rear tyres	21 in.
0–100 km/h (62 mph)	5 sec
Top speed	290 km/h (180 mph)

Jeep Gladiator

Design	Trevor Creed
Engine	2.8 in-line 4 turbo diesel
Power	122 kW (163 bhp)
Torque	400 Nm (295 lb. ft.)
Gearbox	6-speed manual
Installation	Front-engined/four-wheel drive
Front suspension	Multi-link
Rear suspension	Multi-link
Brakes front/rear	Discs/discs
Front tyres	265/75R18
Rear tyres	265/75R18
Length	5207 mm (205 in.)
Width	1947 mm (76.7 in.)
Height	1900 mm (74.8 in.)
Wheelbase	3515 mm (138.4 in.)
Track front/rear	1667/1681 mm (65.6/66.2 in.)
Kerb weight	1882 kg (4149 lb.)

Based largely on the styling of the popular Wrangler, the Jeep Gladiator is a lifestyle pickup, a truck with a strong visual identity and well-understood mechanical credentials. Shown here in open form, it also comes with a canvas roof to protect the load bay. For extreme outdoor feel, the windscreen also folds down and the doors can be removed.

Key elements shared with the basic Jeep models of today are the classic seven-slot grille, an open-air passenger compartment, the 4x4 system, a front winch and skidplates front and rear. The concept still features non-integrated black wheel arches that make the body and chassis appear as two completely separate entities, just as on older pickups. The vertical, side-mounted spare wheel is another throwback to an earlier era.

The cargo bed has the all-important dimensions for a haulage truck: 1.2 metres (4 ft.) wide and up to 2.4 metres (8 ft.) in length. For off-roading, a 348 mm (nearly 14 in.) ground clearance, a 47-degree approach angle and a 38-degree departure angle are useful tough-terrain statistics.

Inside the square and upright cab the seats and interior are weatherproof, allowing them to be hosed out for cleaning. The colour combination is green with dark slate, a tough, outdoor choice; the trim and instrumentation are rudimentary but effective. Contrasting with its utilitarian feel are certain items of modern equipment such as a GPS navigation system and a communications system – "all the necessary technology for finding your way there and getting back", according to Jeep.

The Gladiator name is drawn from Jeep's heritage: the original Gladiator was a full-size pickup model from 1962. The new car is as functional as ever, with that trademark inset cabin protected by the wheel arches and running boards, a feature that reinforces not just the nostalgic feel but also the Jeep go-anywhere ethos.

Jeep Grand Cherokee

Engine	4.7 V8 (3.7 V6 and 5.7 V8 also offered)
Power	172 kW (230 bhp) @ 4700 rpm
Torque	394 Nm (290 lb. ft.) @ 3700 rpm
Gearbox	5-speed automatic
Installation	Front-engined/two- or four-wheel drive
Front suspension	Independent, coils
Rear suspension	Live axle
Brakes front/rear	Discs/discs
Front tyres	235/65HR17
Rear tyres	235/65HR17
Length	4741 mm (186.7 in.)
Width	2139 mm (84.2 in.)
Height	1720 mm (67.7 in.)
Wheelbase	2781 mm (109.5 in.)
Track front/rear	1575/1575 mm (62/62 in.)
Kerb weight	2092 kg (4612 lb.)
0–100 km/h (62 mph)	8.3 sec
Top speed	206 km/h (128 mph)
Fuel consumption	15 l/100 km (18.8 mpg)
CO$_2$ emissions	368 g/km

The Grand Cherokee is the flagship of the Jeep model line-up and something of an American national institution. It was introduced in 1992 and appeared as a second-generation model in 1999; the new 2005 edition, however, is the first produced under the ownership of DaimlerChrysler.

The industry grapevine suggests that it was the division's German chairman who insisted that Jeep's famous seven-slot grille bars return to their original vertical format to reinforce the new Grand Cherokee's boldness and, more importantly, its brand identity. That already-powerful identity is reaffirmed by a very similar overall look to the outgoing model, but with many detailed refinements to give it a more modern feel.

Compared to the previous model there is now a higher waistline that rises in a wedge towards the rear. The most immediately striking change, however, is the move to quadruple round headlights, their curved tops marking the profile of the bonnet's leading edge. Smarter versions have liberal helpings of chrome on the grille, further accentuating the difference. Boxy wheel arches remain a key characteristic of the Jeep's side view, while at the rear large tail lights sweep at an angle into the rear three-quarter panels.

The ground clearance remains high, giving the impression of uncompromising off-road ability. That ability is enhanced with the choice of three different four-wheel-drive systems and – of particular delight to buyers in the USA – the return of the famous Hemi engine as the top, 5.7-litre powerplant. Yet this is still a very sumptuous vehicle, with all-leather upholstery and wood-trim accents expected in the aspiring luxury sector; the dashboard is notably neater and more European in its appearance.

Jeep has clearly played safe with the new Grand Cherokee – understandably so for a core product for which maintaining customer loyalty is more important than pushing the boundaries of engineering and style.

147

Jeep Hurricane

Design	Trevor Creed
Engine	Two 5.7 V8
Power	500 kW (670 bhp) (total)
Torque	1004 Nm (740 lb. ft.) (total)
Gearbox	5-speed automatic
Installation	Front- and rear-engined/four-wheel drive
Front suspension	Short and long arm
Rear suspension	Short and long arm
Brakes front/rear	Discs/discs
Front tyres	305/70R20
Rear tyres	305/70R20
Length	3856 mm (151.8 in.)
Width	2033 mm (80 in.)
Height	1732 mm (68.2 in.)
Wheelbase	2746 mm (108.1 in.)
Track front/rear	1715/1715 mm (67.5/67.5 in.)
Kerb weight	1746 kg (3849 lb.)
0–100 km/h (62 mph)	5 sec

Though only a compact 4.5 metres (15 ft.) in length, the Jeep Hurricane was one of the biggest sensations of the 2005 Detroit show.

An extreme interpretation of everything Jeep and everything 4x4, the Hurricane promises to go where no 4x4 has ever gone before. In effect two Jeeps fused together on the same chassis, the Hurricane has two V8 Hemi engines, one at the front and the other behind the two occupants. Both ends steer, too, not just conventionally but in an astonishing variety of modes that allow the vehicle to perform even more astonishing movements, lending credence to Jeep's claim that it is the most manoeuvrable as well as the most powerful 4x4 ever built.

The Hurricane's most amazing party trick is to turn all four wheels inward and spin round in its own length. The wheels can also all swing to one side, allowing the vehicle to crab out of a space sideways. Conventional countersteering gives a tighter turning circle.

Its style might be highly functional, with many of the mechanical parts exposed to view, but the carbon-fibre chassis concept is sophisticated, with the rudimentary body perched on top. The cockpit uses exposed carbon fibre with polished aluminium, accentuating that lightweight yet extremely strong look.

The overall theme has cues from the Wrangler and the Gladiator but is even more functional looking. There's 363 mm (14 in.) of ground clearance and incredible 64-degree approach and 86-degree departure angles; along with mammoth 37-inch tyres on 20-inch wheels, this allows it to traverse almost any obstacle and climb near-vertical slopes.

Technically clever it may be, but with no visible storage and limited practical utility, it seems this experiment in Jeep branding is destined, like all too many concepts, to remain a glamorous show car rather than to take to the mountain trail.

Kia KCD-II Mesa

Design	Tom Kearns
Engine	3.5 V6
Installation	Front-engined/four-wheel drive
Front tyres	R22
Rear tyres	R22
Wheelbase	2946 mm (116 in.)

The KCD-II Mesa is only the second concept to emerge from Kia's California Design Studio, but it already shows considerable confidence from the fast-growing Korea-based car-maker.

An SUV with the American market set firmly in its sights, the KCD-II is based on a stretched version of Kia's Sorento platform. The exterior design, though it does come complete with the usual rugged look of an SUV, is sufficiently different from existing models to make the KCD-II an interesting vehicle.

Its most noticeable feature is the distinctive 'hard-top' look produced by the narrow windows and low roofline, and by the fact that all the sets of roof pillars are blacked out – apart from the substantial C-pillars, which are rakishly tilted forward. This gives the illusion that it is only these rear pillars that are supporting the roof. The rearmost part of the roof, over the cargo area, is almost all glass, apart from a narrow central metal spine that carries the high-level stop-light at its rear extremity.

There are many different interconnecting shapes at the front that break up the chunkiness and make the vehicle look tough and functional rather than luxurious. Running round the wheel arches is a dark-grey matt band to offer stone-chip protection: this splits as it reaches the sills, to enclose the automatically extending step.

Inside there are six identical bucket seats in three rows of two, each with a sunset-orange back, forming a private individual space for each occupant. Above are twin full-length sunroofs.

Mounted on top of the deep-pressed roof are four alligator-style roof-rack clamps for skis, snowboards and surfboards. The front of the roof also houses an LED searchlight – which Kia suggests could be used for lighting up the waves during a night-time surfing session.

Kia Rio

Engine	1.6 in-line 4
Power	82 kW (110 bhp) @ 6000 rpm
Torque	145 Nm (107 lb. ft.) @ 4500 rpm
Gearbox	5-speed manual
Installation	Front-engined/front-wheel drive
Front suspension	MacPherson strut
Rear suspension	Torsion beam
Brakes front/rear	Discs/drums
Front tyres	175/70R14
Rear tyres	175/70R14
Length	4239 mm (166.9 in.)
Width	1694 mm (66.7 in.)
Height	1471 mm (57.9 in.)
Wheelbase	2499 mm (98.4 in.)
Track front/rear	1471/1461 mm (57.9/57.5 in.)

Kia, a subsidiary of Korea's Hyundai, is one of the most ambitious car companies in the world and in 2004 was by some margin Europe's fastest-growing brand. The new Rio is one of its most important launches ever as it pitches into the busy market for supermini hatchbacks, dominated by the Peugeot 206, the Ford Fiesta and the Renault Clio. In the United States, where only the four-door saloon is to be marketed, the Rio's main rivals will be the Honda Civic and the Toyota Corolla. On both continents the Rio will have a key role in attracting new buyers to the Kia brand.

The outgoing Rio generation was not noted for any particular sense of style: its discreet, rounded shape blended seamlessly into the crowd. The new model, on the other hand, has a stronger character and personality with which to challenge its rivals, though it still steers on the side of caution when compared with the products of, say, Renault.

The new model has a longer wheelbase, wider track and increased power, which give it better ride and handling performance. The front end is designed with a strong V-shaped feature that sweeps out from the number-plate plinth up past the black-meshed grille and triangular headlamps, and on to the bonnet. This has the effect of building visual energy and motion in the car. At the side the doors have tapered rubbing strips that propel the car forward and visually tie the bumpers together.

The hatchback version has an unusual tail-light design, with a clear-glass strip running along the base of the C-pillar and down the inside edge of the lamp where it meets the tailgate. This gives the model a distinctive signature when viewed from the rear – clear evidence, perhaps, that Kia is serious about building a brand identity.

Kia Sedona

Engine	3.8 V6
Power	179 kW (240 bhp)
Torque	339 Nm (250 lb. ft.)
Gearbox	5-speed automatic
Installation	Front-engined/rear-wheel drive
Front suspension	MacPherson strut
Rear suspension	Multi-link
Brakes front/rear	Discs/discs
Front tyres	235/60R17
Rear tyres	235/60R17

Available in showrooms from late 2005, the new Kia Sedona large minivan gave the Korean company's designers a tough challenge: how to update a bestseller, at the same time improving its accommodation, its versatility, its quality and its safety – all the while keeping costs firmly clamped down and ensuring that loyal customers were not alienated.

In responding to such a challenge, something has to give, and in the Sedona's case it is originality and style. The model may perform better on the specification sheet, but in terms of design it offers little or nothing that is new or different.

Thus, apart from the split horizontal grille, it is a struggle to find many distinguishing features on this Sedona that make it stand out from the crowd. The interior, too, comes across as a largely inspiration-free zone – all this points to the Sedona's being a classic case in which designers' ideas have been toned down or even eliminated in the interests of keeping costs and controversy in check.

Instead, it is clear that the latest Sedona is designed to sell on the classic 'soccer-mom' minivan platform of space and specification. There is substantially more room than in the outgoing model and the already high levels of occupant safety are further boosted, according to Kia. And a spectacular equipment list – including the powered, sliding side doors that are now *de rigueur* in North America – ensures it will get directly on to buyers' shortlists.

The new Sedona was conceived largely for the North American market, where it will compete against such vehicles as the Honda Odyssey and the Toyota Sienna. It will also be sold in Asian and European markets and is known as the Carnival in some territories.

Kia Sportage

Engine	2.7 V6 (2.0 in-line 4, and 2.0 diesel, also offered)
Power	129 kW (173 bhp) @ 6000 rpm
Torque	242 Nm (178 lb. ft.) @ 4000 rpm
Gearbox	4-speed automatic
Installation	Front-engined/all-wheel drive
Front suspension	MacPherson strut
Rear suspension	Multi-link
Brakes front/rear	Discs/discs
Front tyres	215/65R16
Rear tyres	215/65R16
Length	4350 mm (171.3 in.)
Width	1800 mm (70.9 in.)
Height	1695 mm (66.7 in.)
Wheelbase	2630 mm (103.5 in.)
Kerb weight	1743 kg (3843 lb.)
0–100 km/h (62 mph)	10.5 sec
Top speed	180 km/h (112 mph)
Fuel consumption	10 l/100 km (28.2 mpg)
CO_2 emissions	237 g/km

The all-new Kia Sportage SUV may have the same name as Kia's outgoing compact 4x4, but that's where the similarity ends. The new model shows a much more global approach and will indeed be sold worldwide (the old car, unusually, was for a while built in Germany, just for European buyers). The new Sportage also offers its customers more choice than the previous model did; there are now three engine options, and the choice of front- or all-wheel drive on the two four-cylinder versions, while two transmissions, two equipment levels and a range of extras make for a much more comprehensive price list.

Although it is one size-class smaller and with a softer edge to its design than the Kia Sorento, the Sportage shares many of its styling themes with its full-size SUV brother. This is a definite plus as the Sorento has been responsible for raising Kia's image in the company's most important markets.

In design terms the Kia's exterior style has classic SUV proportions and uses body-trim elements in a way that has become commonplace on such vehicles. The carlike upper architecture is visually separated from the more rugged lower body as a result. There is good ground clearance and plenty of wheel-to-wheel-arch clearance, suggestive of off-road capabilities. When viewed from the side there is purposeful forward motion generated by the forward-leaning rear screen and the gently rising waistline.

Unusually for an SUV, the tailgate is top-hinged and the spare wheel is carried internally. Usability is a key in SUV design, and for the Sportage, Kia has developed a rear seat folding system that lowers the cushion into the rear footwell so that the backrest folds down to create a square-sided, fully flat-floor cargo area.

Lamborghini Concept S

Design	Luc Donckerwolke
Engine	5.0 V10
Power	373 kW (500 bhp) @ 7800 rpm
Torque	510 Nm (376 lb. ft.) @ 4500 rpm
Gearbox	6-speed manual
Installation	Mid-engined/all-wheel drive
Front suspension	Double wishbone
Rear suspension	Double wishbone
Brakes front/rear	Discs/discs
Front tyres	235/35ZR19
Rear tyres	295/30ZR19
Length	4300 mm (169.3 in.)
Width	1900 mm (74.8 in.)
Wheelbase	2560 mm (100.8 in.)
Track front/rear	1622/1592 mm (63.9/62.7 in.)

The Concept S is a Lamborghini design experiment based on the Gallardo V10 coupé. Its objective is to propel Lamborghini into even more extreme territory, and the most immediately striking difference with the already outrageous standard Gallardo is that there is almost nothing above the car's waistline – neither a roof, nor a windscreen frame, nor even a conventional cockpit.

Instead, the upper half of the car features two separate side-by-side passenger compartments, each with its individual tinted and curved windshield; between the two cockpits the car's upper deck runs flat from the level of the bonnet, the small windscreens allowing a channel of air to run centrally along the deck and be drawn into the large engine air intake at the rear. The loss of the roof emphasizes even more the size of the front air intakes.

As a token feature there is an electrically retractable central rear-view mirror in the upper bodywork; this, as Lamborghini exquisitely phrases it, "allows the driver – when required – to see what is happening behind the car".

Created by Luc Donckerwolke at the Centro Stile Lamborghini in Italy, the Concept S is an extreme expression of Lamborghini styling, with inspiration being drawn from classic single-seater racing cars of the past. Powerful and sleek, the Concept S would be a sensational crowd-puller were it ever to be produced for general sale. It has the allure of a jet fighter aircraft – and no doubt would also feel much like one from either of its dual cockpits.

The Concept S is reminiscent of the Aztec designed in 1987 by Italdesign, and which featured very similar twin windscreens. With no plans for production, the Concept S will remain, like the 350 GTS and the Miura Roadster in the 1960s, Lamborghini's unique expression of extreme open cockpit sensation.

Land Rover Discovery/LR3

Design	David Saddington, Geoff Upex
Engine	4.4 V8 (2.7 V6 diesel also offered)
Power	220 kW (295 bhp) @ 5500 rpm
Torque	425 Nm (313 lb. ft.) @ 4000 rpm
Gearbox	6-speed automatic
Installation	Front-engined/four-wheel drive
Front suspension	Double wishbone, independent
Rear suspension	Double wishbone, independent
Brakes front/rear	Discs/discs
Front tyres	255/55HR19
Rear tyres	255/55HR19
Length	4848 mm (190.9 in.)
Width	1915 mm (75.4 in.)
Height	1891 mm (74.4 in.)
Wheelbase	2885 mm (113.6 in.)
Track front/rear	1605/1612 mm (63.2/63.5 in.)
Kerb weight	2629 kg (5796 lb.)
0–100 km/h (62 mph)	8.2 sec
Top speed	195 km/h (121 mph)
Fuel consumption	15 l/100 km (18.8 mpg)
CO$_2$ emissions	354 g/km

Going under the name Discovery in Europe and LR3 in North America, the third generation of Land Rover's premium family SUV is only the ninth new model in the company's fifty-six-year history. But it's a sorely needed new model, as the outgoing Discovery – paying the price for adopting a look barely distinguishable from the 1988 original – was beginning to appear seriously dated.

Fittingly, the third-generation Discovery is a major step forward, in terms of both visual design and engineering. The new style is as fresh and modern as its predecessor was old-fashioned. Bold geometrical design elements give the longer, wider and lower body a more contemporary look, with the vertical and horizontal theme taking in the three-slat grille, the door shut-lines and handles and the side windows for a smart and highly distinctive look. The rear is again distinctive, featuring an asymmetrically split tailgate that is a thoroughly clever piece of design.

Structurally, too, there is a break with the past: the new model has a unitary body and chassis for better stiffness and improved handling and refinement. The petrol V8 engine is derived from a Jaguar unit, while the new 2.7-litre V6 turbo diesel is a joint Ford–PSA development.

A new patented Terrain Response system maximizes traction over a variety of surfaces. By choosing one of five settings ranging from general driving to mud and ruts or rock crawl, the Discovery driver will always have optimum driveability and control, say Land Rover's engineers.

A great deal of attention has been lavished on the interior, with a fresh, wide dashboard, luxurious leather-upholstered seating and, vitally in this practicality-oriented sector, space for seven occupants. The two rear rows of seats fold flat into the floor.

Designs that, like the Discovery, are updated only at extended intervals need to be well ahead of the game if they are to preserve their momentum in the market. And this third-generation version of the Land Rover classic promises to be just that.

Lexus IS

Engine	2.5 V6 (2.2 in-line 4 diesel also offered)
Power	152 kW (204 bhp) @ 6400 rpm
Torque	250 Nm (184 lb. ft.) @ 3800 rpm
Gearbox	6-speed manual
Installation	Front-engined/rear-wheel drive
Front suspension	Double wishbone
Rear suspension	Multi-link
Brakes front/rear	Discs/discs
Front tyres	205/55R16
Rear tyres	205/55R16
Length	4575 mm (180 in.)
Width	1800 mm (70.9 in.)
Height	1425 mm (56.1 in.)
Wheelbase	2730 mm (107.5 in.)
Track front/rear	1535/1535 mm (60.4/60.4 in.)
Kerb weight	1560 kg (3439 lb.)
0–100 km/h (62 mph)	8.4 sec
Top speed	220 km/h (137 mph)
Fuel consumption	9.3 l/100 km (30 mpg)
CO_2 emissions	222 g/km

L-Finesse, the new design rationale from Lexus, has three fundamental elements: 'Incisive Simplicity' – in effect, product clarity; 'Intriguing Elegance', an appeal to the emotions; and 'Seamless Anticipation', a notion that says the anticipation of an event is fundamental to its ultimate enjoyment. So how does this translate in sheet-metal form in the new IS range, the model that must do battle with classy compact premium saloons such as the BMW 3 Series?

The exterior is unfussy and has strong forms, with a Volvo-esque waistline and an arrowhead D-pillar graphic, a shape that is expected to become a key styling element of all future Lexus models.

The head and tail lamps each form a blunted point and add interest to what could otherwise be fairly conventional front and rear ends; the headlamps are set higher than the grille to enhance the impression of speed, while at the rear, the lamps create a stylistic tension similar to that of an Audi or a BMW. Short overhangs front and rear, together with neatly faired wheel arches with wheels that sit snugly inside, give the IS a sporting and well-planted stature.

As a result the new IS looks strong, dynamic and intriguing, boding well for the growing brand identity being built up by Lexus in a sector where consistent, high-class visual presence is almost a condition of staying in business.

Inside, there are quality finishes and careful attention to detail throughout; some repeat buyers, however, may regret the replacement of the chronometer-style instrument graphics with a more conventional – though undoubtedly classier – display.

The L-Finesse design direction has been explored through the LF-S and LF-C concept cars, and is unquestionably a success on the new IS. And as Lexus's confidence grows, perhaps so too will its courage to go for still bolder front-end designs.

Lexus LF-A

Design	Wahei Hirai
Power	373 kW (500 bhp)
Brakes front/rear	Discs/discs
Front tyres	245/40R19
Rear tyres	285/35R19
Length	4400 mm (173.2 in.)
Width	1860 mm (73.2 in.)
Height	1220 mm (48 in.)
Wheelbase	2580 mm (101.6 in.)
Top speed	322 km/h (200 mph)

Ever since Toyota graduated to Formula One in 2002 it had been on the cards that the Japanese company would wish to build an exotic road car to cash in on the reflected glory of its top-level racing programme. Yet the appearance of the Lexus LF-A at the 2005 Detroit motor show was surprising on several counts. Not only did the car come sooner than expected, but it was wheeled out under the luxury Lexus brand rather than in Toyota's racing colours; perhaps because of this premium branding the LF-A announced itself not as a pure, highly focused supercar like a Ferrari F430, but as a two-seat concept that, according to the company, "blends the performance of an exotic sports car with the luxury refinements of a Lexus".

Not only does the LF-A advance new technologies – though Lexus would not give details of the 500 bhp engine, not even its position within the car – but it also launches a new styling philosophy for the brand, dubbed L-Finesse. As expressed in the LF-A, it is dramatic in the extreme, with strong, elegant proportions, a powerful wedge shape and simple geometric forms. There are no superfluous details cluttering up the body panels: flat and gently twisting planes abound, and the eye is drawn to the play of the light as it reflects off the contours. Even the main air scoops emerge naturally out of the car's shape.

One of the most dramatic views of the LF-A is from the rear, where triple exhausts exit from the central diffuser section, and near-horizontal tail lights sit above massive mesh-covered air outlets with cooling fans clearly visible behind them.

The Ferrari F430 may be aesthetically more refined, but the LF-A is certainly more edgy, more functional – and a good deal more dramatic.

Lexus LF-C

Design	Kevin Hunter
Engine	High output V8
Gearbox	6-speed sequential automatic
Installation	Front-engined/rear-wheel drive
Brakes front/rear	Discs/discs
Front tyres	245/35ZR20
Rear tyres	285/30ZR21
Length	4539 mm (178.7 in.)
Width	1854 mm (73 in.)
Height	1359 mm (53.5 in.)
Wheelbase	2794 mm (110 in.)

Dramatic and eye-catching it most certainly is – edgy and mean-looking, even. The LF-C is the third in a series of Lexus show-car concepts designed to trail new ideas and develop a more exciting visual identity for the upmarket arm of Toyota. Measuring some 4.5 metres (nearly 15 feet) from bumper to bumper, the LF-C has the length of the current IS 200/300 saloon and, says Lexus, points the way to how a future sports coupé off the junior Lexus platform might look.

Though not every designer will agree with the way Lexus has handled the LF-C's coupé-cabriolet shape, there is no denying the impact it delivers. Certainly, some of the panel forms give too much edge and do not sit too comfortably together, and in some lights the feature lines on the sides appear too subtle and allow what should look like an agile coupé to appear overweight. But in other lights the slanting wheel-arch accents show the shape to dramatic effect. The low grille and rounded bonnet rise steeply to the windscreen to create a dramatic wedge-shaped profile, and at the waist there is a vertical surface that sweeps from the front towards the rear, twisting horizontal as it goes.

The interior looks futuristic, with striking contemporary forms and fluorescent green trim to spice up the ambience. The dashboard flows into the high-level centre console, which runs the length of the interior to separate the two sides of the car. Displays and controls are hidden beneath this transparent console surface.

While the heavy proportions of this concept from some angles may seem disappointing, its four-position retractable hard-top is appealing and Lexus's hint that this is a pointer to the future direction of the IS 300 line must be taken seriously. All the same, with a high-power V8 under the bonnet it looks more like a candidate to replace the luxury SC 430 than the lighter, nimbler IS series.

Lincoln Zephyr

Design	David Woodhouse
Engine	3.0 V6
Power	157 kW (210 bhp) @ 6250 rpm
Torque	271 Nm (200 lb. ft.) @ 4750 rpm
Gearbox	6-speed automatic
Installation	Front-engined/front-wheel drive
Front suspension	Short and long arm
Rear suspension	Multi-link
Brakes front/rear	Discs/discs
Front tyres	225/50R17
Rear tyres	225/50R17
Length	4839 mm (190.5 in.)
Width	1834 mm (72.2 in.)
Height	1420 mm (55.9 in.)
Wheelbase	2728 mm (107.4 in.)
Track front/rear	1565/1557 mm (61.6 /61.3 in.)
Kerb weight	1545 kg (3406 lb.)

The Zephyr is the most awaited new model to come from Ford's US luxury division, Lincoln, and as a 2006 model-year compact luxury car it is aimed at the kind of young professional who currently drives a BMW, an Audi or a lower-level Lexus model.

Based on the well-received engineering platform of the Mazda 6 – the Ford group's core component set for entry-level executive models – the Zephyr has something of the Mazda's sporty poise, even though its sheet metal and interior design are entirely different. While the Zephyr stops short of anything radical, its proportions are classically strong and quick to catch the eye. The wheel arches hug the 17-inch wheels and the grille and lamps run horizontally to the outer reaches of the front end, emphasizing the car's width and prowess. At the rear the trapezoidal shapes of the lamps and exhausts are both tastefully proportioned and quietly suggestive of the power on tap.

One of Lincoln's less credible claims is that the interior reflects the European tastes prevalent in its German competitors. The dashboard may be precision-made and incorporate such fine materials as satin aluminium, but the instrument graphics, the lavish use of chrome and the very pale colour choices – even the wood is pale – mark it out as a Detroit product. The interplay between surface textures such as metal, leather and wood is certainly sophisticated and gives a real sense of luxury, but it might not play well outside North America.

Nevertheless, the Zephyr is one of the best new cars to emerge from Lincoln over recent years and is evidence that the Ford group has a new model that is set to mount a credible challenge to the blue-chip nameplates from Germany, Japan and the UK in the entry-level luxury class.

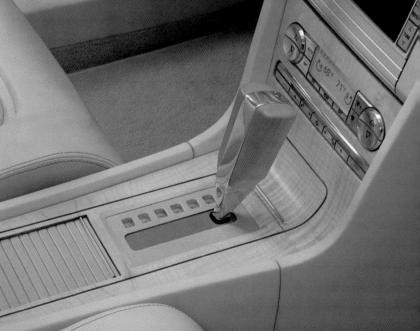

Marcos TSO

Design	Damian McTaggart
Engine	5.7 V8
Power	298 kW (400 bhp) @ 5600 rpm
Torque	508 Nm (374 lb. ft.) @ 4400 rpm
Gearbox	6-speed manual
Installation	Front-engined/rear-wheel drive
Front suspension	MacPherson strut
Rear suspension	Double wishbone
Brakes front/rear	Discs/discs
Front tyres	215/40ZR17
Rear tyres	225/40ZR18
Length	4100 mm (161.4 in.)
Width	1680 mm (66.1 in.)
Height	1150 mm (45.3 in.)
Wheelbase	2290 mm (90.2 in.)
Track front/rear	1450/1400 mm (57.1/55.1 in.)
Kerb weight	1090 kg (2403 lb.)
0–100 km/h (62 mph)	4.0 sec
Top speed	298 km/h (185 mph)

Designed by ex-TVR designer Damian McTaggart, this all-new two-seater British sports car shows a mixture of influences, notably older TVRs and past Marcos GT cars.

The design is classic retro British sports car with a modern twist; a long sweeping bonnet pushes the seats way back in front of the rear wheels, while a strong shoulder line runs the length of the car and lifts, Marcos-style, over the wheels, dropping at the occupant cell and at the tail. The effect is to emphasize the rearward bias and reclined seating position.

At the front there is no bumper but a gaping oval air intake with two narrow body-coloured vertical bands to break up mass. Behind the front wheel is the TSO's most unusual feature: a row of four bright aluminium slatted vents, which lead into a broad bright metal band that extends to the complete door, taking in the rear-view mirror on its way. It is practical, helping to draw air out from the engine bay, and distinctive, hiding the front shut line of the door.

Behind the passenger cell, there is no visible rollover bar: having to add such a feature might compromise the cleanliness of the design, but might be necessary for production. A flat rear deck then slopes away, rising in curvature towards a blunt yet arched rear end in classic Marcos style. The petrol cap is located in a traditional sports car position: in a central spot behind the cockpit opening.

The interior lacks the sophistication of sports cars from the major brands. The Marcos TSO has a wide, symmetrical centre console with white circular dials and flashes of aluminium. A more contemporary interior treatment might have done a more convincing job of showing that Marcos has something genuinely new to offer.

Mazda 5

Design	Moray Callum
Engine	2.0 in-line 4 (1.8, and 2.0 diesel, also offered)
Power	108 kW (145 bhp) @ 6000 rpm
Torque	182 Nm (134 lb. ft.) @ 4500 rpm
Gearbox	6-speed manual
Installation	Front-engined/front-wheel drive
Front suspension	MacPherson strut
Rear suspension	Multi-link
Brakes front/rear	Discs/discs
Front tyres	205/50R17
Rear tyres	205/50R17
Length	4505 mm (177.4 in.)
Width	1755 mm (69.1 in.)
Height	1615 mm (63.9 in.)
Wheelbase	2750 mm (108.3 in.)
Track front/rear	1530/1520 mm (60.2/59.8 in.)

Derived directly from 2003's MX-Flexa concept, the new Mazda 5 replaces the undistinguished Premacy as Mazda's representative in the compact MPV segment – a sector in which competitors' designs are beginning to add exterior stylishness and new levels of interior versatility.

The Mazda 5 looks good on both counts. Based on an extended version of the Ford Focus/C-Max platform, this six- or seven-seater MPV is an attractive and well-proportioned car with a number of interesting design features. Carefully crafted exterior surfaces and an attractive evolution of the new Mazda frontal face give it a distinct style, with the large headlamps wrapping right round over the wheel and bold, high-set tail lamps echoing the theme at the rear.

The passenger side doors are sliding on both sides, so the door handles end up positioned close together to give a good sense of symmetry; the running rail is exceptionally well integrated into the side profile, appearing as one of a number of horizontal lines that run within a smoothly flowing side silhouette. Each of these lines helps to extend the length of the car visually, and the tinted rear side windows add a little sophistication.

There are two exterior specifications, one with chrome accents that emphasize luxury and comfort, the second with side skirtings and tinted lamps that make the centre of gravity appear lower and give a sportier look.

Inside, the six-plus-one seating comprises three rows of two seats, but with a novel twist: a smaller central chair can be folded out of the middle row to provide accommodation for a seventh person – yet in six-seat mode comfort remains uncompromised. Two interior trim options mix strong horizontal and vertical forms for a structured look – and the fact that this new car carries the simple '5' designation means that it is a core model in Mazda's mainstream line-up.

Mazda MX-Crossport

Design	Moray Callum
Installation	Front-engined/all-wheel drive
Brakes front/rear	Discs/discs
Front tyres	275/45R20
Rear tyres	275/45R20
Length	4630 mm (182.3 in.)
Width	1930 mm (76 in.)
Height	1630 mm (64.2 in.)
Wheelbase	2795 mm (110 in.)

The MX-Crossport was designed under the leadership of Moray Callum at Mazda's main design studio in Hiroshima, Japan. In essence, it approaches the new crossover segment from a sporty angle by combining an upper architecture redolent of the Mazda RX-8 sports car with a new lower body in SUV style and with a large, black-meshed front grille and rugged wheels.

Although still a concept, this car is likely to become a showroom reality: Mazda is keen to exploit its current market momentum and, though the Crossport was designed primarily with the North American market in mind, the company is believed to have serious intentions for European sales too.

When the car is viewed from the front, the headlamps sit within the large wheel arches and the bonnet shut line runs from the inside of the lamps to the A-pillars. Along the side windows, the waistline steps up halfway along the rear door while the roofline drops, giving the feel of a more muscular yet aerodynamic shape. The cabin also tapers in at the rear, making the car appear more firmly planted to the ground.

Inside, the feeling of spaciousness is helped by the floating seats, each one secured to the floor via a centrally mounted post. The cabin is very light, a benefit of the panoramic glass roof that comes with a variable control that can change it from clear to translucent white and back again, depending on the light levels required.

The MX-Crossport is a clear sign that strong and attractive design will grow still further in importance for the Mazda brand. The elegant and curvaceous lines of the Crossport will play well with a buying public eager for a crossover SUV with a sports feel but which avoids the aggressive looks that have given 4x4s such a bad image in Europe.

Mazda MX-5

Engine	2.0 in-line 4 (1.8 also offered)
Power	118 kW (158 bhp) @ 6700 rpm
Torque	188 Nm (139 lb. ft.) @ 5000 rpm
Gearbox	6-speed manual
Installation	Front-engined/front-wheel drive
Front suspension	Double wishbone
Rear suspension	Multi-link
Brakes front/rear	Discs/discs
Front tyres	205/50R16
Rear tyres	205/45R17
Length	3995 mm (157.3 in.)
Width	1720 mm (67.7 in.)
Height	1245 mm (49 in.)
Wheelbase	2330 mm (91.7 in.)
Track front/rear	1490/1495 mm (58.7/58.9 in.)

The car world sits up and takes notice when the bestselling two-seat sports car in history is redesigned. So when the all-new, third-generation Mazda MX-5 was presented at the 2005 Geneva Motor Show, car enthusiasts and car designers alike were doubly keen to see how the Japanese company would reinterpret the roadster theme for the twenty-first century.

Redesigning or updating a universally familiar design is a notoriously sensitive task, especially when the existing design is so iconic and so close to people's hearts. Yet the solution developed by Mazda's design team under Moray Callum has elegantly brought the MX-5 bang up to date, to the evident satisfaction of the model's innumerable fans worldwide. The new design is larger, more powerful and more masculine, yet remains faithful to the agile philosophy of the original and, most importantly, is instantly identifiable as an MX-5.

The guiding principle right from the MX-5's earliest beginnings in 1989 was the Japanese concept of *jinba-ittai*, best translated as 'rider and horse as one'. In automotive terms this philosophy means that the driver should be in such close contact with the car that any inputs from one are felt instantaneously by the other.

The new exterior with its smooth surfaces communicates light, agile fun, with new, more pronounced wheel arches giving a more masculine feel than before. Lost in the process is the slight waisting of the body at the doors; greater width is needed to improve interior space and side-impact safety.

The interior design is simple and contemporary, and above all it conveys the right messages for a sports car, with a cocooning tunnel, a neat gear lever and simple, effective switches. Sixteen years after the landmark original, the MX-5's third incarnation does not disappoint.

Mercedes-Benz A-Class

Engine	2.0 in-line 4 turbo (1.5, 1.7 and 1.6, and 1.8 and 2.0 diesel, also offered)
Power	144 kW (193 bhp) @ 5000 rpm
Torque	280 Nm (206 lb. ft.) @ 1800–4850 rpm
Gearbox	6-speed manual
Installation	Front-engined/front-wheel drive
Front suspension	MacPherson strut
Rear suspension	Parabolic rear axle
Brakes front/rear	Discs/discs
Front tyres	195/55R16
Rear tyres	195/55R16
Length	3838 mm (151.1 in.)
Width	1764 mm (69.5 in.)
Height	1595 mm (62.8 in.)
Wheelbase	2568 mm (101.1 in.)
Track front/rear	1552/1547 mm (61.1/60.9 in.)
Kerb weight	1305 kg (2877 lb.)
0–100 km/h (62 mph)	8 sec
Top speed	227 km/h (141 mph)
Fuel consumption	7.9 l/100 km (35.8 mpg)

The original A-Class of 1998 was a dramatically new shape in the small-car class, reflecting its novel technical make-up with its raised double-floor sandwich and near-horizontal engine placement. The new model remains faithful to this layout but is sharper and less playful in its style than the outgoing model. It has grown in length by 232 mm (9 in.) and in width by 45 mm (nearly 2 in.), and as such projects a more powerful stance. From the front, the lamps show more charisma, while from the side the sharper features bring the A-Class right up to date.

The crisp new lines reflect the evolution of other quality German brands, such as BMW. The swage line at the side, starting at the front wheel arch, rises quickly until it reaches the tail light. This line is extremely important as it creates a dynamic feel to what is otherwise a safe and sensible car. The waist-line rises almost as steeply and towards the rear curls up to meet the cant rail, forming the rear side window in the process.

The three- and five-door versions are very cleverly differentiated, the former gaining a sportier look thanks to adjustment of the C-pillar angle and slightly more flare added to the rear wheel arch. It can also be seen clearly how having only one, longer door makes the side view less cluttered, allowing the eye freedom to roam towards the sporty wheels. At the rear, the screen wraps around, visually widening the A-Class, although the crisp design language seen at the side is not so visible at the rear.

The interior is constructed from taut curves and surfaces. The dashboard contrasts open, uncluttered areas with groups of circular and square switches; the overall effect is much classier than the original – which just about sums up Mercedes-Benz's upmarket aspirations for this, its smallest model.

Mercedes-Benz B-Class

Engine	2.0 in-line 4 turbo (1.5 and 1.7, and 2.0 diesel, also offered)
Power	144 kW (193 bhp) @ 5000 rpm
Torque	280 Nm (206 lb. ft.) @ 1800–4850 rpm
Gearbox	6-speed manual
Installation	Front-engined/front-wheel drive
Front suspension	MacPherson strut
Rear suspension	Parabolic rear axle
Brakes front/rear	Discs/discs
Front tyres	205/55R16
Rear tyres	205/55R16
Length	4270 mm (168.1 in.)
Width	1777 mm (70 in.)
Height	1604 mm (63.1 in.)
Wheelbase	2778 mm (109.4 in.)
Track front/rear	1552/1547 mm (61.1/60.9 in.)
Kerb weight	1370 kg (3020 lb.)
0–100 km/h (62 mph)	7.6 sec
Top speed	225 km/h (140 mph)
Fuel consumption	7.9 l/100 km (35.8 mpg)

Mercedes-Benz believes it has identified a potential new segment in the market – that for 'Sports Tourers', sporty, stylish crossovers between sedans, station-wagons and people-carriers. In this strategy the new B-Class, which was previewed at the 2004 Paris show by the CST Vision B concept, sits between the A-Class and the large GST Vision R, with the latter also adding in four-wheel drive to tempt SUV customers.

Despite being based on the front-wheel-drive platform of the A-Class, the B-Class has the commanding presence of a bigger, more luxurious car. There is a calculated similarity with the large GST, with a prominent Mercedes star displayed up front, while the B's size and wedged side profiles combine to make it look both practical and sporty.

The proportions are new to the sector, with a bold front end similar to that found on an SUV, but with conventional ground clearance to anchor the car to the road. The bonnet steps down at the sides to create the arched waistline, and the very tall doors are disguised with strong sporty forms, top, middle and bottom. To help to disguise the vehicle's height, strong horizontal lines accentuate its width.

There is generous space inside, thanks to the sandwich floor construction and the reclining engine under the toe board: this allows 70% of the car's length to be used for either passenger or luggage space. The upper body has large glazed areas to flood the interior with light.

The sporty design language of the Mercedes Sports Tourer family is something quite unique in this sector and could mark the start of an industry trend that puts excitement into practical vehicles.

Mercedes-Benz GST Vision R

Engine	3.0 V6 diesel
Power	163 kW (218 bhp)
Torque	510 Nm (376 lb. ft.) @ 1800 rpm
Gearbox	7-speed automatic
Installation	Front-engined/all-wheel drive
Brakes front/rear	Discs/discs
Front tyres	255/45ZR21
Rear tyres	295/40ZR21
Length	4922 mm (193.8 in.)
Wheelbase	2980 mm (117.3 in.)
Fuel consumption	<9.0 l/100 km (>31.4 mpg)

The Mercedes-Benz Grand Sports Tourer Vision R concept has been several years in the making and is now closer to production than ever. The GST Vision R is not simply a people-carrier or an SUV; it is clearly a unique vehicle that combines MPV practicalities with SUV sporty looks, having four-wheel drive but not extreme off-road ability. This, the third iteration, is the version for Europe, with its wheelbase shortened by 235 mm (9.25 in.) but still with the four-plus-two accommodation of the original.

The front has a deliberate family likeness to the smaller B-class, but thanks to differently shaped headlamps and a less prominent grille it will appeal to a slightly older target market. From the side the form is dynamic, with strongly wedge-shaped proportions and a visual centre that is rearward-biased, culminating in the striking arched side window and a powerful feature line running through into the rear lamp. The wrap-around tailgate at the rear is devoid of much detail, which emphasizes the width and luggage capacity inside. With an external length of almost 5 metres (more than 16 ft.), the GST is extremely spacious inside; six individual seats, with flat-screen monitors for the four rear passengers, transport the passengers in first-class luxury. The seats can be folded and the rear centre console removed in order to carry bulky items such as mountain bikes.

The dashboard features precision-polished aluminium switches and bezels, demonstrating that roomy people-carriers can be equally sporty and luxurious. Light-beige fabrics and olive-green ash wood make for a warm and restful interior.

This is a very spacious and dynamic-looking car that can double up as business, family, shopping and adventure transport. With the smaller A-Class and B-Class, Mercedes is determined to have something for everyone when it comes to stylish, practical people-carriers.

Mercedes-Benz M-Class

Engine	5.0 V8 (3.5 V6, and two 3.0 V6 diesels, also offered)
Power	228 kW (306 bhp) @ 5600 rpm
Torque	460 Nm (339 lb. ft.) @ 2700–4750 rpm
Gearbox	7-speed automatic
Installation	Front-engined/four-wheel drive
Front suspension	Double wishbone
Rear suspension	Multi-link
Brakes front/rear	Discs/discs
Front tyres	255/55R18
Rear tyres	255/55R18
Length	4780 mm (188.2 in.)
Width	1911 mm (75.2 in.)
Height	1815 mm (71.5 in.)
Wheelbase	2915 mm (114.8 in.)
Track front/rear	1619/1621 mm (63.7/63.8 in.)
Kerb weight	2100 kg (4630 lb.)
0–100 km/h (62 mph)	6.9 sec
Top speed	235 km/h (146 mph)
Fuel consumption	13.1 l/100 km (21.5 mpg)

Mercedes-Benz had a lot of ground to make up with the launch of the second generation of its M-Class leisure off-roader. The original model was a big sales success, finding more than 620,000 customers since 1997, but in the intervening years almost every other car-maker has tried to pitch into the same territory and there were aspects of the existing design that were beginning to appear tired or outdated.

A persistent complaint throughout the life of the original model was that its body and interior design were somewhat basic, and that the perceived quality was not up to the high standards expected by Mercedes customers.

The new model, therefore, presents a more sophisticated impression, though it is clearly an evolution of the original theme. Wider, longer and lower than before, it makes a stronger feature of the Mercedes grille and the complex compound headlight assemblies, and its side view is dominated not simply by the characteristic angled C-pillar that visually separates the carlike cabin from the boot, but also by the exaggerated – and again complex – wheel arches. From the rear the blacked-out wrap-around screen helps generate a sense of forward movement, and the rear lights are neatly inset into both the tailgate and the rear wheel arch to link the side and the rear.

The overall effect is at the same time fresh and dynamic and has successfully overcome the simplistic feel of the outgoing model. The transformation is particularly welcome in the cabin, which now comes across as a high-quality luxury environment thanks to noble materials and smooth, clean design. Only the centre-console grab handles provide a clue that this is a machine with off-road ability. Technically, the new M-Class is state of the art, with air suspension, sophisticated traction systems and the option of Mercedes' new diesel V6.

Mercury Meta One

Engine	2.7 V6 diesel-electric hybrid
Power	185 kW (248 bhp) @ 4000 rpm (diesel); 35 kW (electric)
Torque	585 Nm (431 lb. ft.) @ 1900 rpm (diesel only)
Installation	Front-engined/front-wheel drive plus electric rear drive
Front suspension	MacPherson strut
Rear suspension	Multi-link
Brakes front/rear	Discs/discs
Front tyres	255/50R20
Rear tyres	255/50R20
Length	5075 mm (199.8 in.)
Width	1854 mm (73 in.)
Height	1649 mm (64.9 in.)
Wheelbase	2868 mm (112.9 in.)
Track front/rear	1641/1641 mm (64.6/64.6 in.)
Kerb weight	1928 kg (4250 lb.)

The Meta One is described by Mercury as an advanced research concept, but its overall design is sufficiently well resolved to mean that it is likely to serve as the blueprint for the crossover model to be launched in 2007.

The overall proportions and the design elements throughout the exterior are boxy but eye-catching, with very taut surfaces and hard lines; this is taken through to the interior as well. There is a strong horizontal theme that visually widens the car. The headlamps and tail lamps both use LEDs with honeycomb lenses; the light alters in power and direction depending on the car's speed and on the angle of the corner.

High-tech features abound in the Meta One concept. Even the key is a sophisticated device: it stores the driver's personal information and preferences electronically, including seat position, radio station choices and preferred settings for the fully reconfigurable instrument panel that dominates the interior.

This screen runs right across the dashboard and is set into a large, slanting, pale-coloured maple-wood panel that provides a tranquil tone for the whole interior. The display can be used to convey whatever information the driver chooses; when switched off, the screen's translucent orange panels glow in a way that, claim the Mercury designers, echoes the setting sun.

The design of the interior mixes earthy tones with cool blues. Aside from the maple-veneer dash there are polished-aluminium accents and mocha leather for the seats, whose inboard edges rise up to form armrests. The entertainment system has a remarkable fifteen wafer-thin speakers, there is a wi-fi for computer hook-up, and a centre console between the first and second rows of seats has multiple docking stations for music players, DVD games consoles and internet access.

Mercury Milan

Design	Darrell Behmer
Engine	3.0 V6 (2.4 in-line 4 also offered)
Power	157 kW (210 bhp) @ 6250 rpm
Torque	271 Nm (200 lb. ft.) @ 4750 rpm
Gearbox	6-speed automatic
Installation	Front-engined/front-wheel drive
Front suspension	Short and long arm
Rear suspension	Multi-link
Brakes front/rear	Discs/discs
Length	4862 mm (191.4 in.)
Wheelbase	2728 mm (107.4 in.)

Mention of the city of Milan conjures up visions of European fashion, style and sophistication – precisely the kind of associations the US Ford group has in mind for the upscale derivative of the Fusion sedan earmarked for its intermediate, semi-smart brand, Mercury. Thus the Mercury Milan sits between the everyday Fusion and the premium Lincoln Zephyr, all three vehicles sharing the same platform, itself derived from the increasingly ubiquitous architecture of the Mazda 6 – cosmetic engineering in every sense of the term.

The new Milan attempts to set itself apart from the Ford Fusion and Lincoln Zephyr by employing subtle tweaks designed to attract younger buyers and more women. While the underlying mechanical elements are shared across all three brands' contenders, significant differences in the Mercury version's external sheet metal ensure a fresh and individual look. The front – the main area of differentiation – is particularly successful, with wide, dark air intakes below the bumper helping to accentuate the width and stance on the road, and the crisp slatted grille and headlamps contributing to a clean, classy look.

The taut, simple exterior allows the very few satin-aluminium features to stand out, in particular the horizontal strip along the base of the window line that visually lengthens the car. The fourteen-spoke wheels are finely detailed to emphasize a sophisticated product, while the boot and LED rear lights are again different from the standard Ford product.

Inside, too, the Milan uses upscale materials such as satin-aluminium finishers to create an ambience that is at the same time technical and classy; a 'comfort' option specifies warm mahogany wood trim with a two-tone leather interior and contrasting stitching.

An all-wheel-drive option arrives in 2007 and, in tune with Ford's environmental initiative, a hybrid is timetabled to make its debut the following year.

Mitsubishi Eclipse

Design	Dan Sims
Engine	3.8 V6 (2.4 in-line 4 also offered)
Power	194 kW (260 bhp) @ 5750 rpm
Torque	353 Nm (260 lb. ft.) @ 4500 rpm
Gearbox	6-speed manual
Installation	Front-engined/rear-wheel drive
Front suspension	MacPherson strut
Rear suspension	Multi-link
Brakes front/rear	Discs/discs
Front tyres	235/45R18
Rear tyres	235/45R18
Length	4565 mm (179.7 in.)
Width	1835 mm (72.2 in.)
Height	1358 mm (53.5 in.)
Wheelbase	2575 mm (101.4 in.)
Track front/rear	1570/1570 mm (61.8/61.8 in.)

The Eclipse has moved on – but only marginally – since the Concept-E version was first shown at the 2004 Detroit auto show.

The production model still makes a powerful statement but in some of its details it is not quite as extreme. The front air intake has been reduced in size to soften its appearance, while the hybrid power unit is ditched in favour of a 3.8-litre V6 powerplant. From the side, the cabin profile keeps its strong and rakish angle, while the sill section is raised at the rear to almost match the angle of the window baseline.

The overall proportion is still cab-forward, with the roof profile forming a constant arch from front to rear – much like that of an Audi TT, although the Eclipse has a larger boot so the roofline extends further outward at the rear, with surface forms similar in some respects to the Nissan 350Z. To give clear visual reinforcement of the sportier appearance, the wheels are pushed to the four corners; this move is emphasized still more by the large curvature on the front and rear bumpers, which quickly sweep inward from the tyres.

Inside, the layout is fairly plain and simple, with a strong angled wavelike panel running across the dashboard, finished in the exterior body colour to contrast with the predominantly black control zones and centre console. The tunnelled, blue-lit instruments that sit ahead of the driver mimic motorcycle design and make it quite obvious that this is a dedicated sports car that avoids all fussy details.

In its latest incarnation the Eclipse might not be as designer-perfect as some of its competitors, but it promises to provide a serious driver's package that could certainly trouble the likes of the Crossfire, the TT and the Boxster.

Mitsubishi Raider

Engine	4.7 V8 (3.7 V6 also offered)
Power	171 kW (229 bhp) @ 4600 rpm
Torque	394 Nm (290 lb. ft.) @ 3600 rpm
Gearbox	5-speed automatic
Installation	Front-engined/four-wheel drive
Front suspension	Upper and lower A-arms
Rear suspension	Live axle with leaf spring
Brakes front/rear	Discs/discs
Front tyres	275/60R17
Rear tyres	275/60R17
Length	5586 mm (219.9 in.)
Width	1825 mm (71.9 in.)
Height	1742 mm (68.6 in.)
Wheelbase	3335 mm (131.3 in.)
Track front/rear	1594/1598 mm (62.8/62.9 in.)

The Raider is Mitsubishi's new mid-size truck – but its origins are anything but Japanese. It was designed at the Mitsubishi Motors Cypress design studio in California and its engineering is based on that of the Dodge Dakota, a mainstream mid-size truck from the DaimlerChrysler group, of which Mitsubishi once was a member.

With a young target market in mind, the Raider's styling is muscular but not overbearing. The wide-open grille at the front is similar to that featured on other new Mitsubishi models, the aperture turning down at the sides towards the skidplate. The plate itself is highlighted in a lighter colour to make it appear even more massive, a trick repeated with the already large headlamps – which sit on aluminium-trim plinths that seem visually to enlarge their size.

Branded as a performance truck, the Raider has bulges in all the right places, with black trim for rugged appeal running round the wheel arches and bumpers. Buyers can choose from an extended- or double-cab version, and there is an optional 'DuroCross' package that offers a higher ride height, beefier all-terrain tyres, and exterior body enhancements.

The interior comes in either charcoal or khaki colours; although clearly laid out, the Raider's cab fails to rise above the unremarkable standards of other volume-market trucks.

Mitsubishi as a company has been in an increasingly parlous state since the middle of 2004. It needs to stimulate sales, especially in the USA where its fortunes have been in free-fall. The Raider, as a perfectly practical choice in the entry-level truck segment, could be the best chance Mitsubishi has of finding the mainstream success it so desperately needs.

Concept

Nissan Azeal

In its proportions the Nissan Azeal is similar to the Mitsubishi Eclipse. The cab-forward stance of this compact coupé is designed to appeal to young American buyers; it is no coincidence that this is the first Nissan concept car to be shaped at Nissan Design America's new studio in Farmington Hills, Michigan.

In their bid to win the youth vote the designers of the Azeal have picked out the original Datsun 510 and Sentra SE-R as inspirations: minimal overhangs front and rear gave these early Japanese classics a nimble appearance. By moving the cabin forward, the designers have given themselves more flexibility in the roofline treatment. Their solution, a continuous arc back to the broadly flared rear wheel arches, gives the coupé the desired youthful appeal while at the same time separating it usefully in terms of design from many other small cars.

Viewed from the front, a large air intake and wide lower bumper draw the eye down low, making the Azeal seem planted on the ground. The upper grille and headlamps form a subtle V-shape and lead out to the bulging wheel arches. The front wheel arch steps up to the base of the A-pillar, where a separate darker-coloured panel starts its run round the cant rail, emphasizing the arched roof. Individual features, such as the lamps and rear-view mirrors, come in ordered polygon forms with rounded corners.

Inside, the design is very hard, with large machined-aluminium elements and sheer surfaces of dark leather that do little to create a feeling of comfort for the occupants. Nissan may be right in believing it has this concept cleverly pitched at youth buyers, but a little softening of the interior would broaden its appeal considerably.

Design	Mark Milner
Engine	2.5 in-line 4
Gearbox	6-speed manual
Installation	Front-engined

Nissan Tone

Design	Taiji Toyota
Gearbox	5-speed manual
Installation	Front-engined/front-wheel drive
Front suspension	MacPherson strut
Rear suspension	Torsion beam
Brakes front/rear	Discs/discs
Length	4055 mm (159.7 in.)
Width	1705 mm (67.1 in.)
Height	1542 mm (60.7 in.)
Wheelbase	2600 mm (102.4 in.)

Nissan's Tone concept was shown at the Paris show in 2004. Designed at Nissan's main studio in Japan, it nevertheless reflects many of the design cues of the London-designed Qashqai concept featured in the *Car Design Yearbook 3*, as well as the production Micra. In fact it is based on the same Nissan–Renault B platform that underpins both the Micra and the Renault Modus, but a substantial wheelbase stretch to 2600 mm (102 in.) sees it grow into a spacious five-seater, a competitor for much bigger cars and a potential gap-filler between the Micra and the Golf-size Almera.

The new architecture is much more modern and in an almost monovolume style – part mini-MPV and part hatchback. This style provides for a particularly good use of space, as the front occupants can sit higher and further forward, leaving more space behind for rear legroom and luggage. Large doors and low sills give a visual gravity to the Tone as well as making ingress easy. The whole package is aimed at suiting young families who want a fun-looking car that is practical, with strong lines and a striking identity.

The front-end design builds on the bold look of the new Micra, while at the rear the boomerang lamps and triangular side windows follow the well-received Qashqai concept.

Inside, the Tone again reflects the Qashqai, with a deliberately masculine feel, brushed-aluminium features and mainly black trim. The steering-wheel and dashboard design also show Qashqai influence, and a hint of purple radiates through the perforated black and silver leather upholstery to give a sophisticated approach to introducing colour.

Nissan has announced that it will be building the Tone in volume at the Micra's UK plant: much stronger in design than previous mid-market Nissans, it reflects growing confidence in the brand identity around the world.

Nissan Xterra

Engine	4.0 V6
Power	186 kW (250 bhp)
Torque	366 Nm (270 lb. ft.)
Gearbox	6-speed manual or 5-speed automatic
Installation	Front-engined/rear-wheel drive or four-wheel drive
Front suspension	Double wishbone
Rear suspension	Rigid axle, leaf springs
Brakes front/rear	Discs/discs
Front tyres	265/65R17
Rear tyres	265/65R17
Length	4539 mm (178.7 in.)
Width	1849 mm (72.8 in.)
Height	1814 mm (71.4 in.)
Wheelbase	2700 mm (106.3 in.)

Now moving into its second generation, the Xterra is one of a large family of Nissan sport utility vehicles and occupies the position of simple, honest workhorse with a strong emphasis on off-road performance. Others, such as the new Murano, offer more style, while in the USA, where Nissan is a respected name in light trucks, the Titan has been well received as a powerful pickup.

Although the Xterra is a mid-size utility vehicle, the design cues lean clearly towards a no-nonsense off-roader, and as such it sports rugged styling throughout. Everything has certain chunkiness to it, right from the hefty grille bars at the front to the rear bumper complete with its clever integrated sidesteps to help users climb up to reach the roof rack.

The stance of the vehicle gives a clear indication of its purpose, with a raised ground clearance, chunky tyres, and wheel arches with pronounced bulges drawn up high to suggest long suspension travel and cavernous wheel articulation for off-roading. All details are deeply formed to suggest excellent structural stiffness.

Compared to the outgoing model, it has more room, a new 4.0-litre V6 engine, and an all-new, rugged, fully boxed, all-steel chassis based on a modified version of the Nissan F-Alpha platform. The move to rack-and-pinion steering promises improved handling, but the rear suspension remains resolutely basic, with a live axle suspended on leaf springs.

The interior is distinctly carlike but simple and clearly laid out. The colours are kept to the paler end of the spectrum, suggesting comfort, and the aluminium crossbars on the steering wheel pick up the theme of the strong chrome bars on the front grille. Innovative and exciting it is not, but this is not likely to be a handicap in a market where ruggedness and mechanical simplicity are seen as positive qualities.

Nissan Zaroot

Many things are intriguing about Nissan's Zaroot – not least its name, which, say its designers, was chosen as a play on 'the road ahead'.

The design brief for the Zaroot was disarmingly simple: to add sportiness and emotional appeal to an SUV, but not to lose any practicality. In this, Nissan is picking up on a trend launched by the costly Range Rover Sport.

Retaining some of the traditional design cues of an SUV, such as the high stance and large wheels, tyres and wheel arches, the Zaroot departs from the classic formula most dramatically with its full-length gullwing doors. These open upward from hip level; the lower portion hinges downward to provide an entry step. The absence of a B-pillar gives wide-open access to the four-seat cabin.

The long curved door and glass give a dynamic arched profile to the roof, which nevertheless levels off to provide a more practical-looking proportion to the cargo area and the squared-off tail of the vehicle. Viewed from the side, the cabin is clearly differentiated from the load area.

At the front a recessed grille is crossed by twin vertical struts, finished in a contrasting texture, which lead up on to the bonnet. The grille is flanked by distinctive vertical-pillar headlamps, each intersected by a circular lamp unit with the indicator in its rim. Below the bumper is a tough-looking skidplate that clearly signals exciting off-road adventures.

Novel approaches extend to the inside too. The instrument panel has an unusual floating centre console carrying the gear selector, sited just below the central display screen, with a pale orange glow emanating from the instrument backlighting.

Innovative and effective, the Zaroot may perhaps be too extreme for production – but it is sure to be an influence both inside and outside Nissan.

Design	Ryouichi Kuraoka
Installation	Front-engined/four-wheel drive
Front tyres	245/55R20
Rear tyres	245/55R20
Length	4500 mm (177.2 in.)
Width	1800 mm (70.9 in.)
Height	1660 mm (65.4 in.)
Wheelbase	2800 mm (110.2 in.)

Noble M14

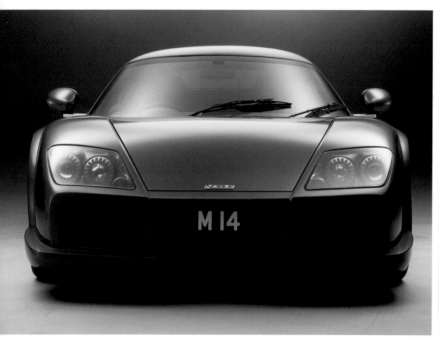

Design	Lee Noble
Engine	3.0 V6
Power	298 kW (400 bhp) @ 6100 rpm
Torque	522 Nm (385 lb. ft.) @ 4750 rpm
Gearbox	6-speed manual
Installation	Mid-engined/rear-wheel drive
Front suspension	Double wishbone
Rear suspension	Double wishbone
Brakes front/rear	Discs/discs
Front tyres	235/40R18
Rear tyres	295/35R18
Length	4267 mm (168 in.)
Width	1935 mm (76.2 in.)
Height	1150 mm (45.3 in.)
Wheelbase	2438 mm (96 in.)
Track front/rear	1570/1550 mm (61.8/61 in.)
Kerb weight	1150 kg (2535 lb.)
0–100 km/h (62 mph)	4.3 sec
Top speed	306 km/h (190 mph)

British specialist sports-car producers have long struggled to achieve credibility against competition from premium brands such as Porsche and Mercedes-Benz: all too often, the UK independents would be full of promise but end up turning out designs that were poorly resolved and low on perceived quality. Noble went some way to correcting this deficiency with its well-received mid-engined M12, with a harmonious style, coherent interior and much-improved reliability.

The M12 earned considerable respect among enthusiasts as an alternative to a TVR, Porsche Boxster or Mercedes SLK. Now Noble is raising its game with the new M14, targeted at a top-end clientele accustomed to driving such exotic machinery as the Porsche 911 Turbo and the Ferrari 360 Modena.

Though the M14 is likely to be technically excellent when production models emerge from the factory, it is always difficult for such a small company to afford the unique parts that give premium models their design edge. Noble has done better than most in attempting to match the exclusive feel of the big-budget Germans, but there is still an unavoidable gulf when it comes to presentation and quality.

The style of the M14 is more brutish than the sophisticated international competition. The soft, domed roof seems at odds with the more edgy lower body; from the side the silhouette is attractive, but the jutting wheel arches and ridged sills interrupt the natural flow of surfaces along the length of the body.

The interior is upholstered in a high-quality mix of burgundy and charcoal leather from the same supplier as Ferrari but, like the exterior, the design does not flow naturally throughout the cabin. Instead, the effect is functional rather than luxurious, perhaps limiting the appeal of the M14 to pure driving enthusiasts rather than those seeking the reassurance of a well-known brand.

Opel/Vauxhall Astra GTC

Design	Martin Smith/Friedhelm Engler
Engine	2.0 in-line 4 turbo
Power	149 kW (200 bhp) @ 5400 rpm
Torque	262 Nm (193 lb. ft.) @ 4200 rpm
Gearbox	6-speed manual
Installation	Front-engined/front-wheel drive
Front suspension	MacPherson strut
Rear suspension	Compound crank axle
Brakes front/rear	Discs/discs
Front tyres	225/45R17
Rear tyres	225/45R17
Length	4288 mm (168.8 in.)
Width	2033 mm (80 in.)
Height	1413 mm (55.6 in.)
Wheelbase	2614 mm (102.9 in.)
Track front/rear	1488/1488 mm (58.6/58.6 in.)
Kerb weight	1210 kg (2668 lb.)
0–100 km/h (62 mph)	8.5 sec
Top speed	234 km/h (145 mph)
Fuel consumption	7.8 l/100 km (36.2 mpg)
CO_2 emissions	223 g/km

The Astra GTC is the production version of the Opel GTC Genève concept shown in March 2003 as a first glimpse of what the all-new Astra line would look like. Since that date the five-door and station-wagon versions have been launched, leaving this sporty-looking coupé version to do double duty as the three-door model for entry-level buyers as well as, in this 2.0-litre turbo form, the performance flagship for the whole Astra line-up.

The powerfully poised, arched profile of the Genève concept is preserved with few alterations for the production version; yet, since its debut two years back, the very linear and razor-edged look no longer seems so fresh – though in today's context it is sure to stand out for its wide, sporty stance and shallow 'low-rider' window line. A very definite standout feature, claimed as a world first, is the optional panorama roof/screen glazing: the windscreen extends right back, over the header rail to the rear passenger area, flooding the interior with light. Complete with shading control, it also offers such practical benefits as being able to look up at traffic lights with ease.

Externally, though the GTC's taut, squat shape is distinctive, it is laden with heavy detailing that some will find excessive. Large headlamps, with individual projector lights against a black background, dominate the front, along with four prominent blacked-out areas and air intakes; the sharply pointed graphics of the side windows and wrap-around tail lights mark out the sides, while the shallow rear window emphasizes the lowness of the glasshouse from the rear. Here, the proportions are visually better but on closer inspection many of the design features seem to serve little or no purpose. The interior, by contrast, is more successful in striking the right balance of sportiness and refinement for its intended customers.

Opel/Vauxhall Tigra

Engine	1.8 in-line 4 (1.4, and 1.3 diesel, also offered)
Power	93 kW (125 bhp) @ 6000 rpm
Torque	165 Nm (122 lb. ft.) @ 4600 rpm
Gearbox	5-speed manual
Installation	Front-engined/front-wheel drive
Front suspension	MacPherson strut
Rear suspension	Torsion beam
Brakes front/rear	Discs/discs
Length	3921 mm (154.4 in.)
Width	1685 mm (66.3 in.)
Height	1364 mm (53.7 in.)
Wheelbase	2491 mm (98.1 in.)
Track front/rear	1429/1400 mm (58.3/55.1 in.)
Kerb weight	1265 kg (2789 lb.)
0–100 km/h (62 mph)	9.4 sec
Top speed	204 km/h (127 mph)
Fuel consumption	7.7 l/100 km (36.7 mpg)
CO_2 emissions	185 g/km

The new Tigra is a thoroughly successful new design that proudly wears the Opel badge in mainland Europe and Vauxhall's emblem in the UK. Like its predecessor of the same name it is a stylish, compact coupé based on the Corsa hatchback platform, but this one has a difference – it is a convertible, too, the rigid roof retracting into the boot in the style pioneered by the Peugeot 206.

Although undisputedly feminine in style, the Tigra is up to date, with edgy design language, big lamps, and wheels pushed right to the corners; thanks also to the all-important folding hard-top, this model has the potential to sell extremely well.

At the front, lines and creases radiate neatly from the centre, though the technical design of the headlamp reflector looks slightly out of place. This type of headlamp styling often looks better with more regular shapes such as rectangles, as seen on the Range Rover. On the Tigra the effect risks looking dated too quickly – it gives a serious look to a vehicle that is supposed to be all about fun.

Apart from this, the Tigra certainly conveys all the right fun-to-drive messages. The strongly wedged proportions and the short, blunted rear end, complete with splayed-M rollover protection and large rear lamps sitting high at the corners, all help to emphasize the fun to be had. Well-defined wheel arches give added sportiness, yet with the skirting below the doors quite restrained, Opel has been able to avoid an overly macho style.

The electro-hydraulic roof is a real highlight and is even available in a contrasting colour to accentuate the hard-top look. Inside there are sporty bucket seats and many sporty accents, particularly all the brushed-aluminium detailing. Unusually, too, the Tigra is available with a diesel engine for the truly cost-conscious open-air enthusiast.

Opel/Vauxhall Zafira

Engine	2.2 in-line 4 (1.6, 1.8 and 2.0, and 2.0 and 2.2 diesel, also offered)
Power	110 kW (147 bhp) @ 5800 rpm
Torque	203 Nm (150 lb. ft.) @ 4000 rpm
Gearbox	5-speed automatic
Installation	Front-engined/front-wheel drive
Front suspension	MacPherson strut
Rear suspension	Torsion beam
Brakes front/rear	Discs/discs
Front tyres	195/65R15
Rear tyres	195/65R15
Length	4317 mm (170 in.)
Width	1742 mm (68.6 in.)
Height	1684 mm (66.3 in.)
Wheelbase	2694 mm (106.1 in.)
Track front/rear	1470/1487 mm (57.9/58.5 in.)
0–100 km/h (62 mph)	11 sec
Top speed	188 km/h (117 mph)
Fuel consumption	8.9 l/100 km (31.7 mpg)
CO_2 emissions	214 g/km

Minivans might not be the most exciting of all the cars featured in the *Car Design Yearbook*: nevertheless, the Zafira does account for 200,000 sales annually and is a very important model to Opel/Vauxhall and its parent company General Motors in Europe.

When the Zafira was first launched in 1997, it featured a seating system that easily folded the five rear seats to create a van-size compartment in the boot. It sold strongly on this versatility, offering the flexibility of seven seats when its competitors could provide only five. More importantly, the seats folded into the floor and did not have to be left behind at home when the Zafira was in cargo mode.

Other manufacturers have now caught up and this feature is no longer a unique selling point. Despite that fact, the updated version has stayed surprisingly close to the outgoing model, though the designers have given the surfaces more volume and updated the look to fit in more comfortably with the latest Astra range, and also to ensure that it meets the latest pedestrian-impact legislation.

The Zafira's body is characterized by crisp lines, but, overall, functionality is the key message: styling is safe, and lots of glass makes for excellent visibility from the all-important raised seating position.

A genuine novelty is the panoramic roof option, which matches four skylight panels alongside a central row of airline-style overhead lockers to store the family's travel paraphernalia. The skylights can be darkened with power-operated shades, and with all the option boxes ticked the specification runs to thirty separate storage compartments. Regrettably, however, the central row of seats still has to be slid forward in order to fold the rearmost row.

Once a leader in its field, the Zafira has regained some lost ground in its second incarnation – but not yet enough to make it first choice in the sector.

Peugeot 1007

Engine	1.6 in-line 4 (1.4 petrol and diesel also offered)
Power	81 kW (109 bhp) @ 5750 rpm
Torque	147 Nm (108 lb. ft.) @ 4000 rpm
Gearbox	2-Tronic automatic and sequential 5-speed
Installation	Front-engined/front-wheel drive
Front suspension	MacPherson strut
Rear suspension	Torsion beam
Brakes front/rear	Discs/discs
Front tyres	185/60HR15
Rear tyres	185/60HR15
Length	3730 mm (146.9 in.)
Width	1825 mm (71.9 in.)
Height	1620 mm (63.8 in.)
Wheelbase	2315 mm (63.4 in.)
Track front/rear	1435/1430 mm (56.5/56.3 in.)
Kerb weight	1145 kg (2524 lb.)
0–100 km/h (62 mph)	12.6 sec
Top speed	190 km/h (118 mph)
Fuel consumption	6.6 l/100 km (42.8 mpg)
CO$_2$ emissions	158 g/km

The Peugeot 1007, presented at the 2004 Paris show, is the production version of the Sésame concept shown two years earlier. The theme remains the same – in particular the sliding doors, which make the 1007 unique among small cars. Several versions of the production model were displayed, along with a high-performance RC concept edition.

The overriding philosophy behind the design of the 1007 is user-friendliness. This comes across in practical terms in the electric sliding doors, operated with either the remote control, the exterior door handle or the interior switches. The arrangement will be especially beneficial in cramped car parks: the fully open door sticks out only 183 mm (7 in.) from the car's side. Also notable are the reconfigurable seats and the interchangeable interior fittings, dubbed 'Camelia' by the company.

Mechanically, the 1007 is based on Peugeot–Citroën's Platform 1, which underpins the Citroën C2 and offers the option of clutchless sequential manual transmission. The sporty 1007 RC concept has a 140 bhp engine and 18-inch wheels.

On all models there is Peugeot's new style of gaping wide air intake bisected by the bumper at the front. This has the effect of disguising the tall proportions that can, if designers are not careful, look top-heavy on a small car. The 'friendly' headlamps, designed in a soft triangular shape, sweep up into the short bonnet towards the base of the windscreen, which then continues in the same plane, up to the roof. Peugeot has been clever with the design of the rear as the waist-rail runner for the door visually continues round on to the tailgate, adding a nice touch of quality.

As shown by its 'double zero' designation, Peugeot sees the 1007 as a niche small car designed to appeal to a restricted market; later, the more mainstream 107, without sliding doors, will take care of the volume market.

Peugeot 107

Engine	1.4 in-line 4 diesel (1.0 petrol also offered)
Power	40 kW (54 bhp) @ 4000 rpm
Torque	130 Nm (96 lb. ft.) @ 1750 rpm
Gearbox	5-speed manual
Installation	Front-engined/front-wheel drive
Front suspension	MacPherson strut
Rear suspension	Torsion beam
Brakes front/rear	Discs/drums
Front tyres	155/65R14
Rear tyres	155/65R14
Length	3430 mm (135 in.)
Width	1630 mm (64.2 in.)
Height	1465 mm (57.7 in.)
Wheelbase	2340 mm (92.1 in.)
Track front/rear	1415/1405 mm (55.7/55.3 in.)
Kerb weight	790 kg (1742 lb.)
Top speed	154 km/h (96 mph)
Fuel consumption	4.1 ltr/100 km (69 mpg)
CO_2 emissions	109 g/km

Peugeot's version of the jointly developed and produced Toyota-PSA small car arrives in the showrooms during 2005, and will replace the 106 as Peugeot's entry-level model in Europe. Manufactured in the Czech Republic using the world-renowned Toyota production system, the 107 will, it goes without saying, be well priced in addition to being well made. The only real question mark is how it will differentiate itself from its two deadliest competitors – the Citroën C1 and the Toyota Aygo, which both happen to originate from exactly the same factory.

All three seek to project a fun, youthful image, important for the urban customer who wants maximum enjoyment at minimum cost, and who often finds parking difficult; and with four proper seats, the common design is practical as well.

Sharing most of its kit of parts with the Citroën C1, the 107 does nevertheless manage to look surprisingly different, especially from the front; most notably, the almond-shaped headlamps draw to a point on the Peugeot version, and there is the large lower air intake with its distinctive wide-mouth look that is now being made the brand signature of the latest Peugeot models.

Perhaps because of this new Peugeot big-mouth identity, the 107 has a more serious facial expression than its Citroën and Toyota equivalents.

The all-glass tailgate at the rear contrasts strongly with the body-coloured bumper, and is a distinctly modern feature. Clever design has helped keep the costs down by minimizing parts variations and production-line complexity – but not at the expense of ending up with a cheap look. There will be three- and five-door versions available, with just a single choice of trim level and two engine alternatives. Again, the overall costs are kept down by minimizing the number of versions available.

Peugeot 907

Engine	6.0 V12
Power	229 kW (500 bhp)
Gearbox	6-speed manual
Installation	Front-engined/rear-wheel drive
Brakes front/rear	Discs/discs
Front tyres	275/40R18
Rear tyres	345/35R18
Length	4370 mm (172.1 in.)
Width	1880 mm (74 in.)
Wheelbase	2500 mm (98.4 in.)
Kerb weight	1400 kg (3086 lb.)

After the recognition Peugeot received when it launched the sporty RC concept in 2002, the company's designers have now gone one step further in producing the V12-powered 907 supercar. But if the general reaction at the concept's Paris unveiling in 2004 is anything to go by, this could have been a step too far.

The 907 immediately projects itself as an outrageous design: a brash, intricate, perhaps even over-designed, upmarket model. But on paper it looks impressive, with 6-litre power and a carbon-fibre body/chassis allowing a light all-up weight of 1400 kg (3086 lb.).

Using classic coupé proportions of the past, the 907 is a mix of old and new. The long bonnet and rearward location of the cab set an overall theme that is unquestionably designed to evoke thoughts of Ferrari. The front is an extreme version of the Peugeot face, with a huge leering grille, a low nose and long headlamps that extend back into the bonnet, making for a streamlined look. To emphasize the V12 power underneath, a glazed panel inset in the bonnet shows off the twelve chromed air intakes; the side vents behind the front wheels are similar to those on the Range Rover and are echoed behind the doors. Below the vents sit Viper-style side-exit exhaust pipes.

There is no hope that Peugeot could ever produce such a car. Its brand could not withstand the price tag and sales would be poor. Ironically, this gives a refreshing freedom to the designers, for whom the 907 could be an uncompromised pure concept intended to capture the attention of the public and media, and to project Peugeot as a more exciting marque. A shame, then, that it is so far removed from the current range that it won't be seen as a serious Peugeot.

Peugeot Quark

Engine	Hydrogen fuel cell
Gearbox	All-wheel drive
Front suspension	Double wishbone
Rear suspension	Double wishbone
Brakes front/rear	Discs/discs
Front tyres	235/45R17
Rear tyres	235/45R17
Length	2380 mm (93.7 in.)
Width	1500 mm (59.1 in.)
Height	1106 mm (43.5 in.)
Wheelbase	1730 mm (68.1 in.)
Track front/rear	1150/1150 mm (45.3/45.3 in.)
Kerb weight	425 kg (937 lb.)
0–100 km/h (62 mph)	6.5 sec
Top speed	110 km/h (68 mph)

Peugeot has gone to unusual lengths in its determination to get people interested and excited about fuel cells. In 2003 the company showed a playful small fire-engine concept called the H2O, based on the 206; now, it has come up with the Quark – not so much a car as an advanced quad.

The Quark carries two people in motorbike-style tandem configuration and is powered by four electric motors, one fitted to each wheel. Peugeot claims that the combination of nickel metal hydride battery and direct-hydrogen fuel cell gives it a range of 130 kilometres (80 miles) before it needs recharging. Hydrogen refuelling is simple thanks to the 'plug and drive' tank – a pressurized canister, holding 9 litres (2.4 gallons) of the liquefied gas, and painted red for easy identification and replacement through the rear.

The all-round hub motors give the Quark permanent four-wheel drive and allow for regenerative braking to conserve energy. The fuel-cell motor is unusual in being air- rather than water-cooled: this, says Peugeot, gets round one of the fuel cell's trickiest problems, that of starting in sub-zero conditions.

Though it is the length of a Smart and seats two, the Quark is visually more quad than car. The high-tech suspension is clearly on show and the miniature mudguards leave bare the revolutionary drive technology underneath. The smiling Peugeot grille, swept headlamps and lion badge are all worked into the front-end design. At the rear the lamp surround appears like a jet engine thrusting Quark along, while a personal-organizer-like 'personal interactive interface' slots into the centre of the handlebars to act as the driver's ignition key, vehicle monitor and navigation assistant.

It may look like a gimmicky plaything, but there is a lot to the Quark's design that is very serious – and that could underpin future fuel-cell models from Peugeot–Citroën.

Pininfarina Birdcage 75th

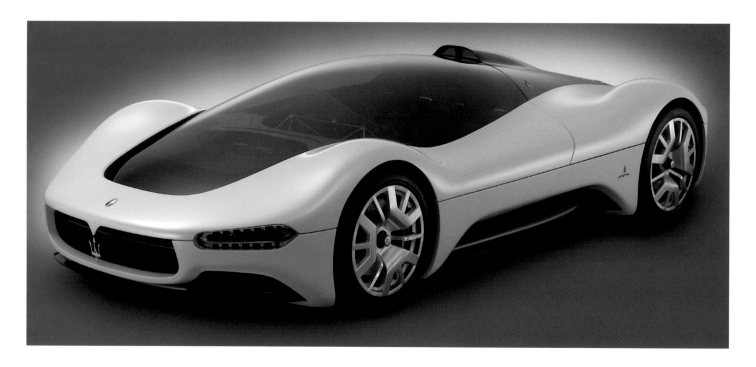

Design	Pininfarina
Engine	6.0 V12
Gearbox	6-speed manual
Installation	Mid-engined/rear-wheel drive
Front suspension	Double wishbone and push rod
Rear suspension	Double wishbone and push rod
Brakes front/rear	Discs/discs
Front tyres	275/30R20
Rear tyres	295/35R22
Length	4656 mm (183.3 in.)
Width	2020 mm (79.5 in.)
Height	1090 mm (42.9 in.)
Track front/rear	1660/1650 mm (65.4/65 in.)
Kerb weight	1500 kg (3307 lb.)

The 2005 Birdcage 75th was launched at the Geneva show to celebrate Pininfarina's seventy-fifth birthday, and is a concept designed around the Maserati heritage.

Positively oozing creativity, the Birdcage 75th is based on the road-racing chassis of the Maserati MC12, itself related to the Ferrari Enzo. Pininfarina's design is beautifully evocative, harking back to racing cars of the 1950s and drawing inspiration from such models as the Maserati A6 GCS of 1954, the Ferrari Dino Berlinetta Speciale, and the Alfa Romeo 33. Yet, despite this array of historical references, the Birdcage – itself named after Maserati's famous sports racer – is every bit as futuristic and forward-looking as its legendary namesake was in the 1960s.

The most striking aspects of the design are its lowness, its width and, especially, the warm fluidity of its every surface. The body hugs the mechanical elements as if a silken cloth had been draped over the structure – a refreshing contrast to the sharp aggressiveness of some contemporary designs. Positively breathtaking is the way the tinted canopy and the white body meet in a sinuous, wavy line that works its way round the car to accentuate the complexities of the surface form.

The low and reclined seating position makes possible a very low roofline, creating a striking proportion. The front has an unmistakable gaping Maserati mouth and piercing horizontal LED headlamps; at the rear the theme is echoed in the very wide tail lights, which have cooling air outlet slots set into them.

The Birdcage 75th has an unusual combination of a supercar architecture and a pure, organic form to create a dynamic tension that serves to make it even more compelling. From the teardrop central mass that encapsulates the passenger cell and the mechanicals to the sensuous shape of the enclosing bodywork, it is just the kind of masterpiece we expect from Pininfarina.

Pininfarina Double-Face

Pininfarina recently acquired Matra Automobile of France, the niche vehicle designer and manufacturer that did a great deal of work for Renault until financial disaster struck.

Double-Face is a joint project between Pininfarina and Matra, aimed not so much at presenting a glamorous style-setting show car as at demonstrating structural and manufacturing techniques to suit today's growing market for niche models derived from a shared, cost-saving vehicle sub-structure. The Double-Face name refers to the idea of developing a mechanical platform capable of accommodating two different body style options, one of steel construction and one made of composite panels.

Disappointingly, however, the two designs are superficially very similar and the advantages of the principle are not immediately clear. The first design, using composite panels, is for an off-road 4x4 SUV coupé, and the second, using steel, is for a more road-going coupé. The former targets a younger market and features different-coloured wheel arches, which contain the small circular headlamps; this leaves the rest of the front-end design rather featureless. The side profile is more masculine, with the big wheel arches and dynamic side window profile. On both variants, the rear lamps blend through into the form of the fender and the rear screen is nicely shaped, the most successful elements of the design by far.

But while both models fall short on aesthetic sophistication, under the surface there is clever engineering thinking. Both, for instance, use an identical steel A-pillar and roof rail, but the greater roof height of the off-road SUV is achieved with a taller C-pillar pressing, a relatively cheap component.

This design is unfortunately not a commercial proposition, and one is left wondering why a more desirable and distinctive shape could not have been chosen to present the technology.

Design	Pininfarina
Installation	Front-engined/four-wheel drive

Pininfarina Nido

Design	Pininfarina
Gearbox	Automatic
Installation	Rear-engined/rear-wheel drive
Front tyres	175/50R16
Rear tyres	205/45R16
Length	2890 mm (113.8 in.)
Width	1674 mm (65.9 in.)
Height	1534 mm (60.4 in.)
Wheelbase	2068 mm (81.4 in.)
Track front/rear	1363/1457 mm (53.7/57.4 in.)

Pininfarina's latest creation, little larger than a Smart, is much more than an engagingly shaped city car. The Italian design and engineering house developed the ingenious Nido (meaning 'nest' in Italian) in response to the industry need for increased levels of safety in small cars. To meet increasingly stringent crash legislation and also to offer more passenger space, many cars are getting larger and heavier, and in comparison smaller cars become more vulnerable on the roads.

The traditional approach to car safety has been to surround a rigid occupant cell with energy-absorbing deformable areas front and rear, and to protect the passengers with active restraint systems such as airbags. But in small cars the amount of energy that can be absorbed is less than in bigger cars, as the front crumple zone is short. This means proportionally greater risk for the occupants, especially when the small car collides with a large car.

Nido's specific innovation is to place a further energy-absorbing layer against the bulkhead between the occupant cell and the chassis structure. This means that in an impact the main chassis absorbs crash energy as usual, but that any remaining energy is dissipated by the sliding forward of the occupant cell by some 350 mm (14 in.), crushing the interconnecting honeycomb absorbers and slowing the deceleration of the occupants. A similar arrangement provides protection in a rear impact. A soft bonnet that conceals the windscreen wipers, and plastic covers for the A-pillars, help to reduce serious injuries to pedestrians.

From an aesthetic viewpoint the Nido is a simple monovolume design with a fun personality. The shape is all-encompassing as if moulded from a single part, and suggests a protective environment. Good visibility is ensured by the large windscreen and windows and the transparent roof.

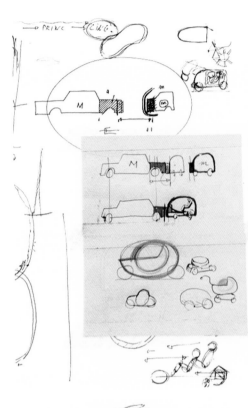

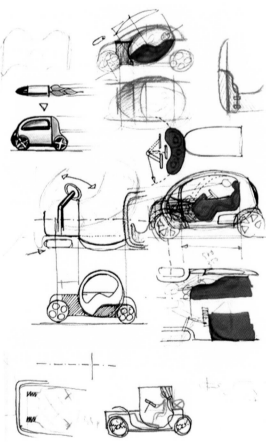

Pontiac Torrent

Engine	3.4 V6
Power	138 kW (185 bhp) @ 5200 rpm
Torque	285 Nm (210 lb. ft.) @ 3800 rpm
Gearbox	5-speed automatic
Installation	Front-engined/all-wheel drive
Front suspension	MacPherson strut
Rear suspension	Four-link independent
Brakes front/rear	Discs/drums
Front tyres	235/65R16
Rear tyres	235/65R16
Length	4795 mm (188.8 in.)
Width	1814 mm (71.4 in.)
Height	1703 mm (67 in.)
Wheelbase	2857 mm (112.5 in.)
Fuel consumption	12.3 l/100 km (23 mpg)

Built on the same architecture as the Chevrolet Equinox and the Saturn Vue, the Pontiac Torrent was launched at the 2005 Greater Los Angeles Auto Show. This SUV – Pontiac's first – is designed as a fun-to-drive fashion statement rather one majoring on real off-road ability. The exterior look is more akin to that of a minivan than an off-roader, with soft radii used all over to give it a friendly and perhaps more feminine feel; nevertheless, key SUV design features include the raised body, tall bonnet and aluminium skidplates front and rear.

Whether intentionally or not, the new design of the twin-frame Pontiac grille lends the Torrent a very BMW-like look at the front.

The five-seater interior is practical, with a highly configurable design that allows the rear chairs not only to recline, but also to slide fore and aft depending on the amount of luggage being carried. Also available for the rear cargo area is an innovative storage system with storage bins in the floor and wheel wells, plus a lightweight polycarbonate shelf with hooks for grocery bags, which can also be reconfigured as a table. Inside, the focus is on comfort and the high level of equipment expected in this segment.

To give the interior an upscale feel and differentiate the Torrent from its Chevrolet and Saturn peers, chrome accents border the instruments (which of course feature Pontiac's signature red backlighting), while tailored seat upholstery runs throughout the cabin. The colouring is sophisticated too, with a mix of dark and paler grey shades to give it a solid and sporty feel.

The Torrent is clearly professionally designed and attractive: the market it joins is crowded yet still profitable, and the model's sporty persona could make it a much-needed success for its GM parent.

Production

Porsche 911

Design	Harm Lagaay
Engine	3.8 flat 6 (3.6 also offered)
Power	261 kW (350 bhp) @ 6600 rpm
Torque	400 Nm (295 lb. ft.) @ 4600 rpm
Gearbox	6-speed manual
Installation	Rear-engined/rear-wheel drive
Front suspension	MacPherson strut
Rear suspension	Multi-link
Brakes front/rear	Discs/discs
Front tyres	235/35ZR19
Rear tyres	295/30ZR19
Length	4427 mm (174.3 in.)
Width	1808 mm (71.2 in.)
Height	1300 mm (51.2 in.)
Wheelbase	2350 mm (92.5 in.)
Kerb weight	1420 kg (3130 lb.)
0–100 km/h (62 mph)	4.8 sec
Top speed	293 km/h (182 mph)
Fuel consumption	11.5 l/100 km (24.6 mpg)
CO_2 emissions	277 g/km

Over the years the Porsche 911 has evolved into the great classic that everyone instantly recognizes. This particular evolution, taking the series to type number 997, is largely a technical and interior development, with what appear to be only fairly minor external alterations – though on closer examination nearly every panel has been changed.

The most obvious change is the return to the more classic oval headlamps, greeted with some relief by owners of the outgoing 996 in which the complex, flat-based lamps were widely regarded as the least successful part of the design. This return to the original Carrera identity is definitely a positive step, which celebrates the 911 in its pure form rather than vainly attempting to modernize a classic.

Wider tracks front and rear make the wheel arches more prominent, emphasizing the slenderness of the 911's waist; thanks to changes to the form at the rear, aerodynamic drag has been reduced from 0.30 to a Cd (coefficient of drag) of 0.28 – a significant achievement considering the need to generate high-speed downforce at the same time.

The engines are 3.6- and 3.8-litre versions of the classic flat six, now of course water-cooled; chassis enhancements, like those to the body, are evolutionary rather than revolutionary.

Inside, the changes are more noticeable. The cabin and dashboard have become more businesslike in their architecture, with a large central navigation screen and the cluster of five instruments in front of the driver now more widely spread apart to enhance clarity. Prominent – if somewhat incongruous – on the top of the dashboard is an analogue/digital stopwatch that allows for the measurement of lap times.

Now stylistically more faithful to the original, this update to the Porsche classic is both sensitive and sensible and has been warmly welcomed by the 911's enthusiastic fan base.

Porsche Boxster

Design	Harm Lagaay
Engine	3.2 flat 6 – S version (2.7 also offered)
Power	209 kW (280 bhp) @ 6200 rpm
Torque	320 Nm (236 lb. ft.) @ 4700–6000 rpm
Gearbox	6-speed manual
Installation	Mid-engined/rear-wheel drive
Front suspension	MacPherson strut
Rear suspension	MacPherson strut
Brakes front/rear	Discs/discs
Front tyres	235/40ZR18
Rear tyres	265/40ZR18
Length	4329 mm (170.4 in.)
Width	1801 mm (70.9 in.)
Height	1295 mm (51 in.)
Wheelbase	2415 mm (95.1 in.)
Track front/rear	1486/1528 mm (58.5/60.2 in.)
Kerb weight	1385 kg (3053 lb.)
0–100 km/h (62 mph)	5.5 sec
Top speed	268 km/h (166 mph)
Fuel consumption	10.4 l/100 km (27.2 mpg)
CO_2 emissions	248 g/km

Porsche has never been a company to make major changes from one model to the next: its preference is to allow its designs to evolve gradually over the years,

The new Boxster follows the same path. As with the pricier 911, the changes are sufficiently minor that, at first glance, the new Boxster appears to be only a face-lift rather than the completely fresh model it actually is. Overall, the changes make the Boxster look more solid and more purposeful: the complex curves, often concave, of the original, are replaced by simpler, bigger surfaces; gone is the delicacy of the first generation.

The front face follows the pattern of the new 911, with oval chrome-rimmed headlamps above the separate integrated indicator and foglamp units. At the rear the dividing line between the rear panel and the body side panels has been lifted to run above the rear lamps, creating an eyebrow impression. Although it is only a small change, this black line has a marked effect of emphasizing the edginess of the rear lamp design and draws the eye upward.

The larger air scoop behind the door marks a definite step up in advertising the Boxster's visual power, yet, along with the flatter, more vertical surface of the door panels, also makes the new car look more like the blocky Toyota MR2.

Larger wheels and wider tracks make for a sportier stance, and Porsche claims better fuel economy and high-speed stability thanks to fully faired underfloor aerodynamic panels – a system that properly manages the airflow under the car.

Inside, the Boxster has grown up very noticeably, abandoning its playful curves and surfaces for a more formal, business-car feel. A notable innovation is the head airbag system for both driver and passenger, the first time this has been achieved in a roadster.

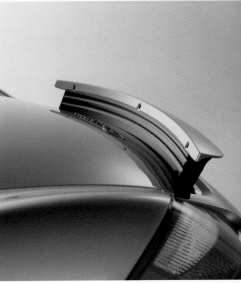

Range Rover Sport

Design	Geoff Upex
Engine	4.2 supercharged V8 (4.4 normally aspirated V8 also offered)
Power	295 kW (390 bhp) @ 5750 rpm
Torque	550 Nm (405 lb. ft.) @ 3500 rpm
Gearbox	6-speed automatic; 2-speed transfer box
Installation	Front-engined/four-wheel drive
Front suspension	Double wishbone, air springs
Rear suspension	Double wishbone, air springs
Brakes front/rear	Discs/discs
Front tyres	20 in.
Rear tyres	20 in.
Length	4788 mm (188.5 in.)
Width	1928 mm (75.9 in.)
Height	1817 mm (71.5 in.)
Wheelbase	2745 mm (108.1 in.)
Kerb weight	2572 kg (5670 lb.)
0–100 km/h (62 mph)	7.6 sec
Top speed	225 km/h (140 mph)
Fuel consumption	15.9 l/100 km (17.8 mpg)
CO_2 emissions	374 g/km

Range Rover lovers were given a real treat at the Detroit show in 2005 with the launch of the new Range Rover Sport, seen as an evolution of the Range Stormer concept shown the previous year, albeit far less radical a design.

The name Range Rover Sport suggests a higher-powered and style-tweaked version of the Range Rover, but instead it is a completely new fifth model, which is joining the Land Rover line-up. Although this naming policy is at first slightly confusing, it is clear to see how and why Land Rover is using the kudos of the top-premium Range Rover brand to drive the marketing, rather than establishing a completely new name.

The Range Rover Sport is a performance SUV, which means its design and chassis settings are optimized for better on-road handling and touring comfort. The Sport is consequently built lower than its larger brother and comes with a calibration of its dynamic response suspension that is firmer than that on the family-oriented Discovery. The result is less body-roll on-road, and thus more positive handling. The suspension can naturally be switched out of its firm on-road mode when venturing off the highway, allowing greater wheel articulation and traction.

In terms of design, although it shares no exterior panels with the Range Rover, the Sport has clear Range Rover proportions and shares the family resemblance. An easy distinguishing point is the air outlet in the front fender. Inside, the cabin is very driver-focused, with a high centre console bringing the many controls within easy reach, and an arched instrument binnacle that protects the instruments from glare.

It is a long time since Range Rovers were simply transport for farmers. But now, remarkably, the Range Rover Sport means that Range Rovers can appeal to wealthy racy types too.

Renault Fluence

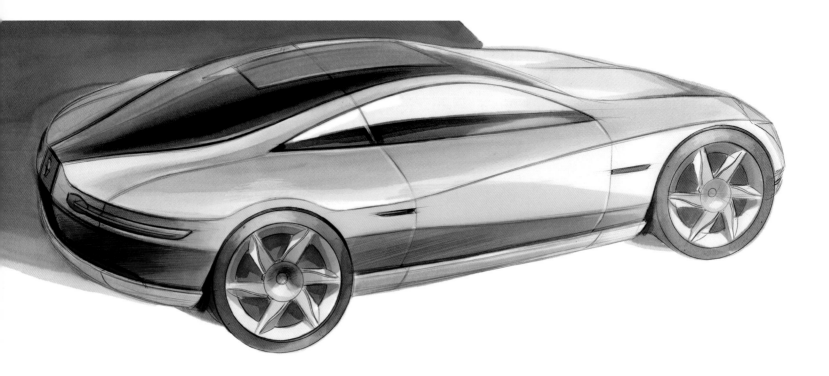

The Renault Fluence was unveiled to the public at the 2004 Louis Vuitton Classic, a prestigious event held at Waddesdon Manor, near Oxford in England. Renault had launched the Initiale at a similar event in 1995 and clearly values the fact that the cars are viewed outside in natural light with plenty of space around them.

The Fluence is a fine four-seater sports coupé, crafted in well-established proportions, but with elegant and attractive detail to make it special. When the car is viewed from the side, the high waist and unfussy panels give the shape an inherent strength, while the tyre-hugging wheel arches, fast windscreen and sloping rear screen make it look low and streamlined. Two feature lines run in a converging manner from front to rear, the upper one coming from the apex of the headlamp and gradually falling across the door to meet the rear lamp, briefly highlighting the rear wheel arch on its way. The lower of the two lines begins from the bumper and gradually sweeps upward and rearward until it too reaches the rear lamp.

The front is dominated by the grille-less bonnet, focusing attention on the Renault diamond logo, and with LED lighting nestling into the wheel arches. The back is very different, with surfaces, lines and a vertical dark panel all culminating in the middle to form the centre stop-light on the edge of the tailgate.

The tailgate itself is interesting, opening upward and forward in a parallelogram movement so as to minimize the height of the open door. Inside, the seats are conceptual shell-like structures with central mountings that allow more legroom for the passengers.

Instrumentation is decidedly minimalist, adding to the impression that this elegant, futuristic design will need a more realistic interior if it is to go into production.

Design	Patrick le Quément
Engine	3.5 V6
Power	209 kW (280 bhp)
Gearbox	6-speed automatic
Installation	Front-engined/front-wheel drive
Length	4600 mm (181.1 in.)

Renault Modus

Design	Patrick le Quément
Engine	1.6 in-line 4 (1.2 and 1.4, and 1.5 diesel, also offered)
Power	73 kW (98 bhp) @ 5700 rpm
Torque	127 Nm (94 lb. ft.) @ 4250 rpm
Gearbox	5-speed manual
Installation	Front-engined/front-wheel drive
Front suspension	MacPherson strut
Rear suspension	Torsion beam
Brakes front/rear	Discs/discs
Front tyres	185/60R15
Rear tyres	185/60R15
Length	3792 mm (149.3 in.)
Width	1695 mm (66.7 in.)
Height	1589 mm (62.6 in.)
Wheelbase	2482 mm (97.7 in.)
Track front/rear	1471/1450 mm (57.9/57.1 in.)
Kerb weight	1160 kg (2557 lb.)
0–100 km/h (62 mph)	11.4 sec
Top speed	177 km/h (110 mph)
Fuel consumption	6.7 l/100 km (42.2 mpg)
CO_2 emissions	161 g/km

As the most strongly design-driven of the volume car producers, Renault has a history of presenting imaginative, mould-breaking concept cars and turning them into big successes in the market-place. Now launched as a production model virtually unchanged from the concept, the Modus is just such a car and clearly demonstrates Renault's mission to provide a Scenic-style breakthrough in versatility in the smaller, supermini-size class.

Compared with the concept, the all-glass roof is reduced in size so that it can open electrically, and a further novelty is added in the shape of the 'boot-chute' – a separately hinged panel in the tailgate that allows access to the boot in confined spaces. It also allows boot access when yet another novelty – the ingenious 'Velofix' bike rack, extending out from the rear bumper – is in use.

The Modus's upright, cab-forward style allows generous interior space. At the front the wide, smiling air intake and big headlamps carry an arch up on to the base of the windscreen that splits up the A-pillar and along the doors, leaving a crisp feature line that runs in an arc through the door handles as it moves rearward. The tail lamps are circular and fun, while the boot steps out slightly, in the typical new Renault style. The waistline is kept low, leaving a large glazed area to make the cabin bright; inside, the rear seats not only fold and slide forward and back, but also switch from a three-seat bench to twin chairs at the pull of a lever. Few cars are as inventive in their accommodation.

The Modus has the charm and charisma to endear it to the female market on emotional grounds alone – but such is its ingenuity that its appeal will extend to modern families too. And, like the Scenic before it, the Modus could surprise even Renault in the number of buyers it attracts.

Renault Zoé

Design	Patrick le Quément
Engine	1.2 in-line 4
Power	75 kW (100 bhp)
Torque	145 Nm (107 lb. ft.) @ 3000–4000 rpm
Gearbox	5-speed automated manual
Installation	Front-engined/front-wheel drive
Brakes front/rear	Discs/discs
Front tyres	225/40ZR18
Rear tyres	225/40ZR18
Length	3450 mm (135.8 in.)
Width	1680 mm (66.1 in.)
Height	1420 mm (55.9 in.)
Wheelbase	2245 mm (88.4 in.)
Track front/rear	1475/1475 mm (58.1/58.1 in.)
Kerb weight	950 kg (2094 lb.)
CO$_2$ emissions	140 g/km

Renault's latest concept car, the Zoé, is an upper-range urban vehicle with compact proportions but retaining appealing and dynamic style. Designed for city driving, when a car on average carries just 1.4 people, the Zoé is a dedicated three-seater with a boot located directly behind the driver's seat. The replacement of the fourth seat by a boot space allows adequate luggage volume for three people.

The Zoé features cheerful rounded forms with a blend of sharp creases. The glass concentration in the upper architecture visually lightens the upper body and adds to the modern feel of the overall design. The body is asymmetrical, with a motorized sliding rear door on one side only to give easy access to the rear seat. To further improve access to the interior, the glazed side section of the roof lifts up when one of the doors is opened. The two glass roof panels are inlaid with LEDs to provide gentle interior illumination when travelling after dark by reproducing the starry canopy of the night-time sky.

A particular Zoé innovation, unique in this class, is its 'Pass' system. The Pass is a small portable device like a Palm organizer, but which, when slotted into its dock by the steering column, automatically adjusts the interior ambience to match each individual driver's tastes in music, climate, and seat and mirror positions.

Other practical space-saving features include a tailgate where the rear window and tailgate slide into one another when swung open to keep the overall height to a minimum. In addition, the small left rear window can be lowered so small items can be easily placed on the parcel shelf – itself a novel mesh structure – or in the boot. The satin-aluminium speedometer appears freely suspended on a glass plaque and, like the whole inspired design, brims with confidence and originality.

Rinspeed Senso

Engine	3.2 flat 6
Power	186 kW (250 bhp) @ 6200 rpm
Torque	300 Nm (221 lb. ft.) @ 4600 rpm
Gearbox	6-speed manual
Installation	Rear-wheel drive
Front suspension	MacPherson strut
Rear suspension	MacPherson strut
Brakes front/rear	Discs/discs
Front tyres	235/35R19
Rear tyres	255/35R19
Length	4475 mm (176.2 in.)
Width	1820 mm (71.7 in.)
Height	1200 mm (47.2 in.)
Wheelbase	2415 mm (95.1 in.)
Track front/rear	1595/1560 mm (62.8/61.4 in.)
Kerb weight	1385 kg (3053 lb.)
0–100 km/h (62 mph)	5.9 sec
Top speed	250 km/h (155 mph)

Yet another outlandish concept from Swiss firm Rinspeed, the Senso explores new relationships between driver and vehicle by orienting its whole design and operation around the driver. Whatever happens, the driver is the focal point in every way.

Described as the most sensuous car in the world, the Senso can sense the driver's biometric state by measuring his or her heart rate and driving behaviour. The Senso then exerts what is claimed to be a positive effect on the driver's mental and physical state by using patterns, colours, music and fragrances. The rationale is that a person who is relaxed and wide awake simply drives better and more safely.

The Senso puts the driver in the centre, flanked by two passengers. Carbon-fibre parts are used both in the interior and for the exterior to give the car a technical look. The driver's ears are stimulated by sounds played through a digital media store on a computer. The nose is also stimulated, by scents being pumped in through the car's air-conditioning vents. Vanilla-mandarin is supposed to exert a calming effect, while citrus-grapefruit is more stimulating. Should the central computer recognize any symptoms of tiredness in the driver, electric motors integrated in the seat will shake him or her awake by vibrating.

Yet it might have been wiser for Rinspeed to have designed the Senso's exterior to create a more calming reaction in the first place. Instead, the car has heavy, unbalanced proportions and is covered from top to bottom with jutting shapes and sharp short lines for minimum harmony and maximum stress. Rinspeed claims the exterior design takes inspiration from the world of architecture: perhaps taking inspiration from the Taj Mahal rather than Manhattan skyscrapers would have been more appropriate.

Reassuringly consistent, Rinspeed once again brings new off-the-wall ideas to Geneva. Also reassuring is the fact that the Senso will never reach production.

Saab 9-7X

Design	Michael Mauer
Engine	5.3 V8 (4.2 in-line 6 also offered)
Power	224 kW (300 bhp) @ 5200 rpm
Torque	448 Nm (330 lb. ft.) @ 4000 rpm
Gearbox	4-speed automatic
Installation	Front-engined/all-wheel drive
Front suspension	Double wishbone
Rear suspension	5-link live axle
Brakes front/rear	Discs/discs
Front tyres	255/55R18
Rear tyres	255/55R18
Length	4912 mm (193.4 in.)
Wheelbase	2869 mm (113 in.)
0–100 km/h (62 mph)	7.8 sec
Top speed	191 km/h (119 mph)
Fuel consumption	13.7 l/100 km (16.5 US mpg)

The Saab brand enjoys a particular place in the hearts of connoisseurs of car design: the Swedish marque is renowned for going its own way when it comes to shaping not only its engineering and its interior detailing, but its external style too.

So it was with some horror that Saab enthusiasts learned that the Saab label, famed for its individuality, was to be applied to two existing mainstream products from General Motors' extended family in order to boost showroom traffic in the USA and ensure Saab customers stayed loyal to the brand. The first was a Saab version of the Japanese Subaru Impreza hatchback, while the second is this Saab take on the American Chevrolet TrailBlazer, a mid-size SUV.

Few vehicles could have been further from the popular idea of a Saab than a V8 truck built on GM's GMT360 platform. But on the evidence of the 9-7X, Saab's chief designer at the time, Michael Mauer, has done a masterly job in applying the Saab look and feel to the once-butch monster truck. Gone are the heavy, jacked-up look and the boxy contours: Mauer's version blends in the Saab corporate nose with exceptional skill, creating the look of a low-set, clean-living station-wagon. Only from its raised rear does the Chevy look become evident.

It ranks as an equal achievement to have given the 9-7X an interior that successfully lifts the US–Swedish product into something a Saab owner would be comfortable in: the dashboard is in the familiar ergonomic Saab style and there is even the centre-console location for the ignition key.

It is likely to be an even tougher challenge for Saab and GM's engineers to give this US-inspired, US-built off-roader, with its clunky engineering, the driving characteristics that Saab customers expect. But one thing is for certain: in design terms Saab's first-ever SUV is much more successful than anyone had dared to hope.

Saturn Aura

The Saturn Aura makes no secret of the external influences in its design: in fact, parent company General Motors makes a big play of the Aura's 'European' exterior and how it showcases the styling direction for future Saturn vehicles.

The European influence in question is that of the Opel Vectra, the vehicle from which the Aura has been evolved. Nevertheless, the design – which is billed as a concept but which will most likely become a mainstream product – is somewhat Audi-esque in its side profile and has a strong C-pillar, a high waistline and a long, spacious-looking cabin. The body makes effective use of its well-defined creases and surfaces to reflect and pick up the light falling from above, the gradually rising waistline and the slightly flared lower skirting catching the light and emphasizing the horizontal lines that suggest a relaxed longitudinal movement.

At the front, large headlamps sandwich the wide chrome bar that holds the Saturn badge, now larger and more confident. The lower bumper grilles are matched in proportion with the upper air intake and again look European.

At the rear a centre crease is just noticeable on the boot lid, echoing the same detailing on the bonnet. The centrally mounted twin exhausts and the small lip spoiler on the boot give a discreet sporty touch. The rear looks slightly more American than the front, thanks to the heavy-looking bumper that sweeps up at the edges.

Inside, there is a fairly standard layout with little design innovation: instead the focus is on using leather and titanium for a luxury feel. There is so much more potential to be innovative with interiors and it is a pity this is not exploited more. Nevertheless, the Aura is a big move towards stronger design for Saturn and has been well received in the USA.

Design	GM Design and Performance Division
Engine	3.6 V6
Power	190 kW (255 bhp) @ 6200 rpm
Torque	346 Nm (255 lb. ft.) @ 3200 rpm
Gearbox	6-speed automatic
Installation	Front-engined/front-wheel drive
Front suspension	MacPherson strut
Rear suspension	Multi-link
Brakes front/rear	Discs/discs
Front tyres	245/40ZR19
Rear tyres	245/40ZR19
Length	4871 mm (191.8 in.)
Width	1829 mm (72 in.)
Height	1448 mm (57 in.)
Track front/rear	1565/1575 mm (61.6/62 in.)

Saturn Sky

Design	Ed Welburn
Engine	2.4 in-line 4
Power	127 kW (170 bhp) @ 6400 rpm
Torque	220 Nm (162 lb. ft.) @ 4800 rpm
Gearbox	5-speed manual
Installation	Front-engined/rear-wheel drive
Front suspension	Short and long arm
Rear suspension	Short and long arm
Brakes front/rear	Discs/discs
Front tyres	245/45R18
Rear tyres	245/45R18
Length	4091 mm (161.1 in.)
Width	1813 mm (71.4 in.)
Height	1274 mm (50.2 in.)
Wheelbase	2415 mm (95.1 in.)
Track front/rear	1543/1561 mm (60.7/61.5 in.)
Kerb weight	1300 kg (2866 lb.)

Due for production in 2006, the Saturn Sky is a compact and affordable roadster with its sights set on the iconic Mazda MX-5. Unusually, it was inspired by the Vauxhall VX Lightning concept that was created at General Motors' Advanced Design Studio in Birmingham, England.

There is space for two occupants, seated rear of centre in the classic front-engined, rear-wheel-drive sports car format. Behind the occupants are two racing-inspired panel bulges that slope down from the headrests. Viewed from the front, the two pairs of lamps rise up towards the outside, making a clearly sporty statement. At the top of the headlamps a ridge is created that sweeps in an arc to the front of the door; this is then picked up again on the rear wheel arch, terminating at the rear lamp.

The doors have flow lines that extend along from the forward air vent, and that gradually fade out. At the rear the lamps are set high up, appearing to give the Sky a sense of forward motion even when sat still. The wheel arches bulge to emphasize the tyres and their connection to the road. There is a folding convertible roof that stows away neatly in the rear under a clamshell cover.

Inside, the space is tight and highly focused on the driver's needs. A high centre console carries a sporty, short-travel gear lever and its large aluminium surround, and there are neat black switches on the console in the centre of the predominantly black- and red-finished dashboard – just one of the available colour schemes.

All in all, Sky is a very attractive roadster that will boost interest in Saturn – but it will still have to compete with GM's own Pontiac Solstice as well as with the new Mazda MX-5.

Seat Leon

Design	Walter de' Silva
Engine	2.0 in-line 4
Power	149 kW (200 bhp) @ 5100–5600 rpm
Gearbox	6-speed DSG manual
Installation	Front-engined/front-wheel drive
Brakes front/rear	Discs/discs
Front tyres	265/30R19
Rear tyres	265/30R19
0–100 km/h (62 mph)	6.9 sec
Top speed	236 km/h (163 mph)

Seat has been talking the talk over the past few years about how it plans to raise the sporty character of its brand and fuse this with a strong Latin flair so as to compete head-on with Alfa Romeo.

The much-praised Salsa concept of 2000 became the launch pad for the latest styling direction: cleverly, it combined the concepts of hatchback, coupé and compact minivan in one intriguing shape. The Salsa ethos guided the design of the next production models that followed – the Altea and the Toledo. Yet there was an unspoken sense of disappointment that the odd proportions of these models had not truly reflected the Salsa spirit. Seat, it was felt, could do more and could do better.

It was left to a surprise entry at the 2005 Geneva show to prove that point. The new Leon, shown in high-performance concept form at Geneva and set for volume production later in the year, is the most dynamic of the three Salsa-inspired designs and the one that best captures the essence of the Salsa.

Like the Altea and Toledo, the Leon is based on the new Golf platform, and its front-end design is familiar from those two models, too. Yet its character is very much sportier thanks to lower general build and a greater sense of being solidly planted on the road. The Leon's sporty character is further accentuated by its dynamic C-pillar and its coupé-like rear door, complete with the Alfa-style handle set above the waistline.

Notable exterior features include the strong shoulder line, the large meshed air intakes in the front bumper and the windscreen wipers that park vertically against the A-pillar. The curved feature line that runs from the headlamp rearward and down through the doors has become a unique Seat hallmark.

Seat Toledo

Engine	2.0 in-line 4 (1.6, and 1.9 and 2.0 diesel, also offered)
Power	112 kW (150 bhp) @ 6000 rpm
Torque	200 Nm (147 lb. ft.) @ 3500 rpm
Gearbox	6-speed manual
Installation	Front-engined/front-wheel drive
Front suspension	MacPherson strut
Rear suspension	Multi-link
Brakes front/rear	Discs/discs
Front tyres	205/55R16
Rear tyres	205/55R16
Length	4458 mm (175.5 in.)
Width	1768 mm (69.6 in.)
Height	1568 mm (61.7 in.)
Wheelbase	2578 mm (101.5 in.)
Track front/rear	1534/1523 mm (60.4/60 in.)
Kerb weight	1472 kg (3245 lb.)
0–100 km/h (62 mph)	9.7 sec
Top speed	206 km/h (128 mph)
Fuel consumption	8.3 l/100 km (34 mpg)
CO$_2$ emissions	200 g/km

The third-generation Toledo marks a brave second step for Seat in its strategy to develop a dramatically different style for what was once a conservative, downmarket cousin of Volkswagen. Now under Audi brand leadership, Seat is looking to become smarter, sportier and more individual, leaving Skoda to fill the gap for affordable blue-collar motoring.

Like the Altea compact MPV, the Toledo has the distinctive new Seat nose; where the two differ most strikingly is at the rear. The longer Toledo, reflecting its role as a more luxurious saloon-car substitute, has a dramatic wrap-around rear screen and a stepped-out boot. The effect is very much like that of recent Renaults, especially the large Vel Satis saloon and, to a lesser extent, the Mégane hatchback. The former has not sold strongly but the latter is doing very well, so the omens for Seat are mixed.

As with the Altea, itself directly derived from the Salsa concept, a sweeping dynamic line runs from the headlamp and over the front wheel and gradually descends to the rear wheel arch. The high-sided silhouette is as deliberate as the cat's-eye headlamps and the well-formed curves that run across the Toledo's body. The rear presents a broad, blank face, high-lipped and framed by relatively conventional-looking tail lights. The lack of extraneous detail helps to focus attention on the large central Seat badge that doubles as the tailgate latch.

The interior mixes black trim with white button markings and aluminium embellishments. Although sporty and with some fun elements worked into the design, the cabin shows less vision than the exterior.

With the Toledo, Seat has achieved a dramatic and evocative design with flair and a Mediterranean personality, which will please those who appreciate unusual and avant-garde shapes, but which, equally, risks alienating the more conservative buyer.

Sivax Xtile

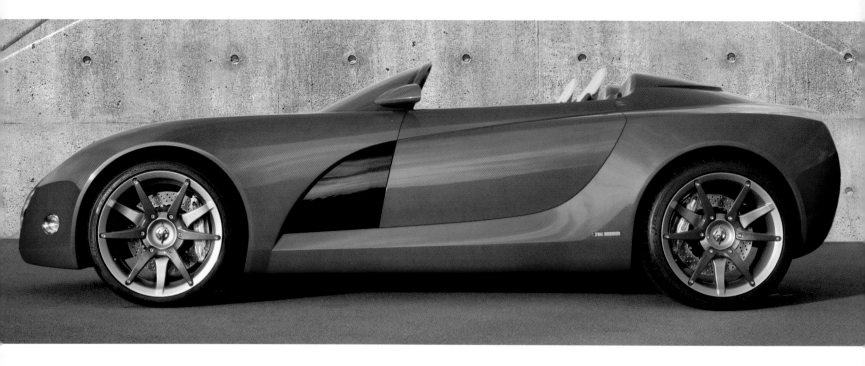

Design	Sivax Design Team
Gearbox	6-speed manual
Installation	Front-engined/rear-wheel drive
Front suspension	Double wishbone
Rear suspension	Double wishbone
Brakes front/rear	Discs/discs
Front tyres	225/35R19
Rear tyres	225/35R19
Length	4000 mm (157.5 in.)
Width	1880 mm (74 in.)
Height	1120 mm (44.1 in.)
Wheelbase	2400 mm (94.5 in.)
Track front/rear	1570/1610 mm (61.8/63.4 in.)

The Xtile follows on from the lacklustre Kira featured in the *Car Design Yearbook 2*, and is a much more successful design from Japanese style house Sivax. As a two-seater roadster the Xtile exploits established principles such as the interplay of surfaces and the merging of exterior and interior, but the new design is more resolved and less naïve by far; it appears to be a car that is much closer to a production possibility than before.

The Xtile has strong proportions, with large wheels pushed right to the extremities and a high waistline that cocoons the occupants. A small wrap-around windscreen and retro-style bulges behind the headrests combine to focus the attention clearly on the driver, who sits midway between the front and rear wheels. When the car is viewed from the side, the main styling feature comes from the dramatic curve that rises up from the sill, through the door, and then rolls round the boot lid. Behind the front wing, the black sail panel helps to break up the body colour, emphasizes the curve and also hints at the dark power that lurks in the engine bay.

The headlamp units rise up as they are drawn rearward, accentuating the length of the bonnet; this is an undeniably strong feature that will leave people's opinions divided. The rear lamps by comparison are nicely set in a bright-metal surround, and the whole back, complete with diffuser aerodynamics, is well proportioned and attractive.

The doors open with a parallelogram action, and, inside, the main feature is the central bar that separates the occupants. This is certainly a unique feature, echoing the sweeping curve on the exterior; nevertheless, it would pose many practical problems in use.

This could be just the concept to give Sivax's automotive and product design valuable credibility in the market-place.

Skoda Yeti

The Yeti represents an evolution of the thinking behind the Skoda Roomster concept, shown to some acclaim in 2004; the model shown at Geneva in 2005 has much greater feasibility for production, though no build decision has yet been taken.

In any conventional segmentation of the market based on vehicle length and width, the Yeti fits between what the Volkswagen group labels the A0 and the A segments – roughly, between the Polo and the new, built-in-Brazil Fox. Yet in its configuration it is much more like a Renault Kangoo or a Fiat Panda than the neat, tidy VW hatchbacks.

The Roomster concept had a distinctive wrap-around windscreen, a darkened A-pillar and the characteristic clam-roof covering. These have all been transferred across to the Yeti, and a white roof with black roof rails has been added to increase its playfulness. The overall design is young and friendly, with a cheerful front-end arrangement that conveys a chunky feel at the same time. Round headlights inset between the rectangular main units and the black bumper corners project a tough, rugged impression, as does the metal-finish skidplate that protects the front apron.

The square proportion, the strong shoulders and the black cladding round the car's sides and on its corners all reinforce the impression of a solid and stable vehicle.

The interior incorporates some interesting design ideas that go beyond the basic feature content. For instance, all the controls are large so that they can be used even when wearing gloves, and there is a cooled water container in the centre console with two removable drinking tubes – an idea taken from the world of cycling.

While the name Yeti has obvious connotations of exploration off the beaten track, this is in reality a city car that might make the occasional trip to the beach.

Design	Thomas Ingenlath
Length	3820 mm (150.4 in.)
Height	1579 mm (62.2 in.)
Wheelbase	2465 mm (97 in.)

Stola S86 Diamante

The S86 Diamante is intended by Stola as a demonstration of its prototype-model-making capability. The Stola group has a long history, originally as a model-maker for the foundry and automotive industries, then making one-off prototype bodies for Italian car companies. During the 1970s Stola expanded its business to provide production tooling capability for car bodies and eventually a full-scale body engineering and production service for niche vehicles.

The S86 Diamante is a static model that Stola claims was designed and made in just five weeks. It takes its name from the eighty-six years the company has been in business. Marcello Gandini, famous for Lamborghinis such as the Miura, has managed to design a car that is not like any specific brand, but which has Italian signifiers that demonstrate a high level of body complexity and feasibility, and is also suggestive of a future design.

In terms of proportions this two-seater has a bias towards the rear; this is further emphasized by the tension created in the body side panel by its intersecting surfaces and the slim and visually independent C-pillar. The heavy front and rear ends give the design an American feel; for its part, the recessed door panel provides a strong Italian connection, but, perhaps for good reason, the odd, angled kink of the side feature line over the rear wheel arch is a feature not seen on any other vehicle.

The interior is bright, contrasting orange with black panels, and provides an eye-catching look. Unfortunately, as a design that is poorly resolved, the S86 tends to grab attention for all the wrong reasons. In the process Stola may have proved its engineering prowess by building the S86 in five weeks, but it has also proved that good design needs rather longer.

Design	Marcello Gandini
Length	4275 mm (168.3 in.)
Width	1930 mm (76 in.)
Height	1225 mm (48.2 in.)
Wheelbase	2600 mm (102.4 in.)
Track front/rear	1535/1555 mm (60.4/61.2 in.)

Subaru B9 Tribeca

Engine	3.0 flat 6
Power	186 kW (250 bhp) @ 6600 rpm
Torque	297 Nm (219 lb. ft.) @ 4200 rpm
Gearbox	5-speed automatic
Installation	Front-engined/four-wheel drive
Brakes front/rear	Discs/discs
Front tyres	255/55R18
Rear tyres	255/55R18
Length	4822 mm (189.8 in.)
Width	1878 mm (73.9 in.)
Height	1686 mm (66.4 in.)
Wheelbase	2749 mm (108.2 in.)
Kerb weight	1925 kg (4244 lb.)

Subaru has long had a reputation for outstanding four-wheel-drive cars, but until now its expertise has been only applied to smaller sedans, station-wagons and hatchbacks. So, surprisingly, the Tribeca is the Japanese brand's first proper SUV – its first venture into a booming market segment that dovetails so well with Subaru technology.

The new vehicle's name will be more familiar to Americans than to those elsewhere, for Tribeca is well known to New Yorkers as a vibrant and progressive neighbourhood filled with boutiques, galleries and restaurants. This is clearly an aspirational choice of name for an aspirational model targeting a design-conscious American clientele.

Design therefore plays a strong role in the image the Tribeca projects. The new three-part Subaru grille design, already shown in the small R2 in Japan and the B9 Scrambler roadster concept car, is the most prominent feature of the Tribeca; unfortunately, its very horizontal form and slats suit the roadster rather better than this much taller SUV body. The front end appears to recline backward and looks too weak for the vehicle's overall size. The Porsche Cayenne suffers a similar handicap; the Range Rover, by comparison, looks much better balanced.

Viewed from the side, a unique Subaru feature does however differentiate the Tribeca from other SUVs. A V-shaped ridge runs from the rear door towards the rear lamp, growing in size as it travels, and wraps round into an Alfa-like tail-light cluster to form a ridge across the tailgate. This attractive effect is marred by the excess complexity of a recessed lower panel that exaggerates the tall, bulky look.

The Tribeca may mark a more adventurous policy for Subaru, but sadly the progress is not in a direction that will make it attractive to the style-conscious customers now calling the shots in the SUV sector.

Suzuki Concept X

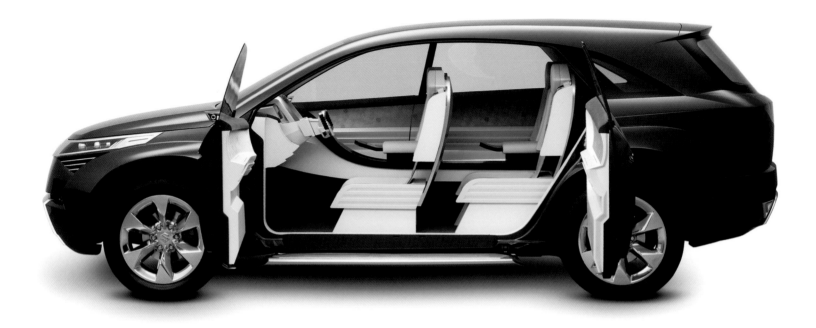

Engine	3.6 V6
Gearbox	5-speed automatic
Installation	Front-engined/four-wheel drive
Front tyres	265/50R20
Rear tyres	265/50R20
Length	4996 mm (196.7 in.)
Width	1834 mm (72.2 in.)
Height	1750 mm (68.9 in.)
Wheelbase	2858 mm (112.5 in.)

The Concept X is Suzuki's first medium-large SUV. Its classic SUV proportions are made all the more striking by the prominent bonnet extending well forward of the massive blistered wheel arches: the bonnet is almost semicircular in plan and is smoothly rounded in side-view, too, giving the effect of a large boat.

There is no frontal grille as such, just a narrow, undecorated slot where the smooth bonnet meets the large bright-metal skidplate that serves as a front bumper; 1930s-style air vents adorn the high sides of the bonnet and sit directly below the strong metallic band running round the front and incorporating the LED headlamps at its outer edge. The side features twin doors that open wide outward from the centre to leave broad access to the interior, unobstructed by a B-pillar.

The upper body gradually tapers as it runs rearward, a neat touch that creates spaciousness at the front and a sporty feel at the rear. Typical SUV features include a reprise of the satin silver chrome under-guard theme on the sides, where the guards serve as retractable steps, and at the rear.

Suzuki's combination of razor-edge styling with more bulbous surfaces and panels succeeds in creating visual tension, but the look is far too extreme for what is necessary. The interior comes across as too much of a designer's dream vision, too, with white angular surfaces rather than a solution that is in any way practical for an SUV.

Suzuki is planning to build an evolution of the Concept X for 2006. This is a sensible policy, as the current concept is too radical to be feasible for production – triangular exhaust tailpipes being just a single example.

Suzuki Swift

Engine	1.5 in-line 4 (1.3 also offered)
Power	75 kW (101 bhp) @ 5900 rpm
Torque	133 Nm (98 lb. ft.) @ 4100 rpm
Gearbox	5-speed manual
Installation	Front-engined/front-wheel drive
Front suspension	MacPherson strut
Rear suspension	Torsion beam
Brakes front/rear	Discs/drums
Front tyres	185/60R15
Rear tyres	185/60R15
Length	3695 mm (145.5 in.)
Width	1690 mm (66.5 in.)
Height	1510 mm (59.4 in.)
Wheelbase	2390 mm (94.1 in.)
Track front/rear	1470/1480 mm (57.9/58.3 in.)
Kerb weight	1075 kg (2370 lb.)
0–100 km/h (62 mph)	10.0 sec
Top speed	185 km/h (115 mph)
Fuel consumption	6.5 l/100 km (43 mpg)
CO_2 emissions	159 g/km

The new Swift has been taking shape slowly over the past few years, with design elements first being shown on the Concept S in Paris in 2002, and on the Concept S2 unveiled at Frankfurt in 2003. The production version has been slightly toned down from the concept to widen its appeal.

Japanese design often focuses first and foremost on the needs of the home market, but the designers and engineers on the Swift programme kept a strong focus on Europe as the main market. A 'one-and-a-half box' proportion was chosen for the Swift, making it look more classic than monovolume in shape, the style often adopted for vehicles in the supermini sector.

Its strong shoulder line, crowned (curved) roof and chunky black pillars give it a generally solid and grounded look. At the front the wide rectangular grille is mirrored by an air intake lower down and, coupled with the large, clear headlamps, it gives a sporty feel. The flared wheel arches and the pronounced shoulder line that leads to an inset upper architecture give the Swift its stable appearance. At the rear the tailgate lip cuts into the bumper, which in turn incorporates horizontal feature lines that extend to the far extremes of the car, accentuating its width. The strong C-pillar and small roof spoiler, with high-mounted stop-light, ensure that from the rear the Swift is recognized as a sporty model. The interior is simple and continues the sporty feel, which will no doubt appeal to the younger market.

Overall, the Swift marks a major departure for the normally conservative Suzuki; in some ways it conveys a similar external feel to the Mini and could pick up some customers in search of a lower-cost alternative to the BMW-inspired product.

Tata Xover

Installation	Front-engined/four-wheel drive
Front suspension	Double wishbone
Rear suspension	Multi-link
Brakes front/rear	Discs/discs
Length	4850 mm (190.9 in.)
Width	1920 mm (75.6 in.)
Height	1800 mm (70.9 in.)
Wheelbase	2850 mm (112.2 in.)

India is not noted for car design, but has enormous potential in its car market as the growing economy mobilizes huge numbers of buyers. And Tata, India's largest car-maker, is uniquely positioned to exploit not only this nascent domestic demand but also South-East Asia's markets in general, as well as other territories further afield, such as Europe. Already Tata sells its Indica and Indigo small cars in southern Europe, and in an ultimately unsuccessful collaboration it provided an adapted Indica for sale by MG Rover under the Cityrover label.

India's mix of poor road quality and high vehicle occupancy levels has prompted the development of the Xover which, as its name perhaps implies, is configured as a crossover between a people-carrier, a station-wagon and a rugged SUV. It is unusual among crossovers in using a separate chassis frame – Tata has much experience with SUVs using this type of structure – in order to endow it with the ruggedness to cope with difficult road conditions.

And with half an eye on eventual exports to more style-conscious markets, Tata engaged the services of Italy's noted I.De.A design institute for the shaping of the body.

The result is a tall, smoothly shaped design that has the contours of a large, passenger-carrying minivan such as the Mitsubishi Grandis. SUV cues are notably absent: the car sits far too low to the ground to be a plausible off-roader, and the wheels and tyres are too modest.

In aesthetic terms the Xover is only a qualified success, appearing bulky and slab-sided despite original design solutions at both front and rear and an interesting profile to the window line and the D-pillar. New technologies include LED front and rear lighting, PC screens and keyboards in the seat backs for work on the move, and four-zone air-conditioning inside the seven-seat cabin.

Toyota Avalon

Design	Ian Cartabiano
Engine	3.5 V6
Power	209 kW (280 bhp) @ 6200 rpm
Torque	353 Nm (260 lb. ft.) @ 4700 rpm
Gearbox	5-speed automatic
Installation	Front-engined/front-wheel drive
Front suspension	MacPherson strut
Rear suspension	MacPherson strut
Brakes front/rear	Discs/discs
Front tyres	215/55R17
Rear tyres	215/55R17
Length	5009 mm (197.2 in.)
Width	1849 mm (72.8 in.)
Height	1486 mm (58.5 in.)
Wheelbase	2819 mm (111 in.)
Track front/rear	1580/1565 mm (62.2/61.6 in.)
Kerb weight	1583 kg (3490 lb.)
0–100 km/h (62 mph)	6.6 sec
Fuel consumption	9 l/100 km (26 US mpg)

The all-new Avalon was launched at the Detroit show in January 2005. It is Toyota's flagship sedan in the USA and serves as big brother to the Camry, itself a regular contender for the nation's top-seller slot.

Despite its size, the Avalon lacks visual presence; the model line's market position has always been a conservative one, and the new edition carries on that tradition. The front-end design fails to project the prestige image of comparable top-line cars from other brands: even though the headlamps and grille look great on their own, the combined chemistry is not quite there. The side is more successful, with a long cabin, an elegant feature line that runs from the headlamps to the tail lamps, and a triangular C-pillar. Nevertheless, long overhangs at front and, especially, rear contribute to a bulky, ponderous look.

The interior has a certain prestige feel to it: it is kept smooth, clean and non-technical, with leather and walnut giving the quality element and surfaces flowing calmly into one another to keep the occupants feeling rested. The climate control system will retain the owner's preferred settings for cabin temperature and air distribution, while useful electrical innovations include an LED turn signal that is mounted at the edge of the door mirrors, and LED puddle lamps that light the ground alongside the car as passengers approach.

Also available as an option is a laser-controlled cruise system that detects slower vehicles travelling ahead and automatically decreases speed accordingly. There is also a remote engine starter so the driver can start the engine from a remote location by depressing a button on the keyfob.

Toyota's technical record is second to none, but in this instance the company would have been wiser to have aimed for greater distinction when honing the Avalon's exterior design.

OBJECTS IN MIRROR ARE
CLOSER THAN THEY APPEAR

Toyota Aygo

Engine	1.0 in-line 3
Power	50 kW (68 bhp) @ 6000 rpm
Torque	93 Nm (69 lb. ft.) @ 3600 rpm
Gearbox	5-speed manual
Installation	Front-engined/front-wheel drive
Front suspension	MacPherson strut
Rear suspension	Torsion beam
Brakes front/rear	Discs/drums
Front tyres	155/65R14
Rear tyres	155/65R14
Length	3405 mm (134.1 in.)
Width	1615 mm (63.6 in.)
Height	1465 mm (57.7 in.)
Wheelbase	2340 mm (92.1 in.)
Track front/rear	1420/1410 mm (55.9/55.5 in.)
Kerb weight	790 kg (1742 lb.)
0–100 km/h (62 mph)	14.2 sec
Top speed	157 km/h (98 mph)
Fuel consumption	4.6 l/100 km (61.4 mpg)
CO_2 emissions	109 g/km

With its name derived from the two syllables 'I' and 'go', the Aygo is Toyota's take on the new city car jointly developed with Peugeot and Citroën. The name, says Toyota, symbolizes freedom and mobility – a description that could prove very apt given the new car's low price, its youthful presentation and its promise of responsive about-town handling.

Sharing its engineering platform and many other components with the Citroën C1 and the Peugeot 107, the Toyota nevertheless manages to be the most expressive and most attractive of the three. Its unique front and rear treatments are an important element in this differentiation.

At the front a smiling Yaris-like face gives the Aygo a friendlier expression than the equivalent Peugeot's large, leering grille and oversized, pushed-back headlamps; at the rear, likewise, the Toyota's more horizontally oriented lamp blocks look more grown-up than the French-branded car's vertical strips. The Toyota's rear lights are drawn forward into the rear quarter-panel, which is again different from those on the Citroën and the Peugeot, necessitating a different door pressing on five-door versions.

The Aygo is designed as a hip urban vehicle, with a marketing campaign focusing on several major European cities, rather than a country-by-country approach. The average customer is expected to be young and new to the Toyota brand. Low prices are key for this market, and the design of the Aygo and its two sister cars is ingenious in the way it is able to simplify the car's make-up to take out cost but at the same time ensure that Toyota's exemplary standards of fit, finish and quality are upheld.

For example, the number of body panel variations is minimized and all three versions share a common interior that focuses on fun and enjoyment. Despite this commonality, however, the Toyota cleverly manages to appear that crucial cut above the rest.

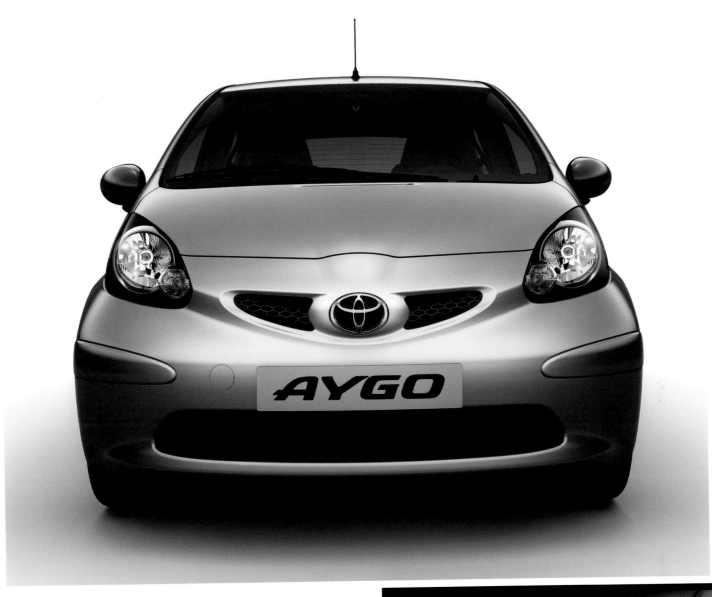

Toyota FJ Cruiser

Engine	4.0 V6
Power	163 kW (245 bhp)
Torque	383 Nm (282 lb. ft.)
Gearbox	6-speed manual
Installation	Front-engined/four-wheel drive
Brakes front/rear	Discs/discs
Front tyres	265/70R17
Rear tyres	265/70R17
Length	4511 mm (177.6 in.)
Width	1895 mm (74.6 in.)
Height	1801 mm (70.9 in.)
Wheelbase	2690 mm (105.9 in.)

Visitors to the 2005 Chicago Auto Show might have felt a sense of *déjà vu* when approaching the Toyota booth. Such a sensation was entirely intended for, resplendent in bright blue with a white roof, the 2006 FJ Cruiser is a direct development of the 2003 Detroit show FJ concept, itself harking back to the iconic Land Cruiser series of the 1960s.

So positive was the feedback surrounding the 2003 concept that Toyota has turned it into a production version that will be available at Toyota dealerships in early 2006. Encouragingly, the design sticks faithfully to the spirit of that highly appealing concept: even the much-talked-about triple wind-screen wipers are carried across intact.

The FJ's design theme is best described as mildly retro, with a basically modern shape given historical significance by the skilful use of design cues from earlier Toyota off-road models. The most noticeable of these is the thick, polished-metal grille surround enclosing round headlights at either end, with the Toyota name picked out centrally in chrome letters on the black mesh background: this is pure '60s Land Cruiser. So, too, are the angular cutouts to the wheel arches, the relatively upright windscreen (though less so on the production car than on the concept) and the wrap-around rear corner windows.

Yet the overall configuration of the FJ Cruiser is much more in keeping with modern demands than the narrow, boxy and upright original. It looks longer, wider and more solid in its stance, and the massive sides, thick pillars and narrow window apertures give something of the impregnable allure of a Hummer. However, the FJ has nowhere near the intimidation factor of the army-inspired US product: its image is much friendlier, more youthful and, ultimately, more appealing.

Toyota FT-SX

Design	Ian Cartabiano
Engine	3.5 V6
Front tyres	255/45R21
Rear tyres	255/45R21
Length	4760 mm (187.4 in.)
Width	1890 mm (74.4 in.)
Height	1549 mm (61 in.)
Wheelbase	2900 mm (114.2 in.)

Created at Toyota's Calty design centre in Newport Beach, California, the FT-SX is the Japanese company's expression of what a future luxury sports-wagon crossover might be like.

The exterior of the FT-SX is undeniably bold, especially the large slab-sided doors blending into the pronounced front and rear wheel arches. The front grille slats are also extremely imposing, as are the LED headlamps, the whole impression accentuated by a bonnet kept relatively featureless so as not to provide distraction. The roofline is slightly arched and the waistline high, again giving a sporty impression.

The FT-SX is a strongly proportioned design combining car-based SUV and sedan cues with sharply defined features and broad haunches. Sitting low on 21-inch wheels, the body hugs the tyres and uses powerfully tight surfaces. At the rear the tailgate is visually very heavy and its technical complexity, with three different opening options, would make it difficult to productionize. An innovative glass roof has two panels that slide towards the centre to create a sunroof effect.

The interior is truly innovative, with a mix of colours, materials and textures, such as cork, leather and aluminium, and high-finish wood accents on the console and outboard of each bucket-style seat. The driver's instruments wrap round the steering column in a boomerang shape, and are clearly not for sharing.

Certain details would undoubtedly need changing should the FT-SX ever become a production model: division bars would have to be added in the side windows to allow the glass to drop into the doors, the door mirrors would have to be made bigger to improve the rear visibility, and the tailgate would have to be simplified.

This is certainly a concept worthy of high regard – even if it comes across as a mite too bullish for Toyota's current market position.

Tramontana

Design	Josep Rubau
Engine	5.5 V12
Power	373 kW (500 bhp)
Torque	825 Nm (608 lb. ft.)
Gearbox	6-speed manual
Installation	Mid-engined/rear-wheel drive
Front suspension	Double wishbone
Rear suspension	Double wishbone
Brakes front/rear	Discs/discs
Front tyres	315/30R18
Rear tyres	335/30R18
Length	4900 mm (192.9 in.)
Width	2070 mm (81.5 in.)
Height	1200 mm (47.2 in.)
Kerb weight	950 kg (2094 lb.)
0–100 km/h (62 mph)	4 sec
Top speed	300 km/h (186 mph)

A graduate of London's Royal College of Art, Josep Rubau has seen his fantasy come true – or at least a big part of it. Rubau's dream had been to design his own car and launch it at an international motor show, which was precisely what happened when he presented his Tramontana two-seater at the Geneva Motor Show in 2005.

But it is after this all-too-brief moment of glory that the real challenge comes: how to turn the single show car into a production enterprise that will turn a profit. Even with an expected selling price of £210,000 for the eventual vehicle, the engineering and investment hurdles are daunting.

Drawing inspiration from jet fighter aircraft, Rubau set about building what was in effect a Formula One car for the road. It took him six years to develop the Tramontana; now, he is thinking in terms of a limited production run of twelve units a year. Based on the Costa Brava in Spain, Rubau, a former VW engineer, has used aerospace techniques to develop a carbon-fibre chassis and part-aluminium body-work. The fighter-plane and F1 thinking is clearly evident in the tandem seating position, the exposed suspension and the large side air intake pods, though these are so massive that they make the body look heavy in comparison to the wheels.

The canopy swings forward like a door to allow for easier access to the cockpits, although entry and exit are still going to require a carefully practised series of moves.

The name Tramontana refers to 'a cold dry wind that blows south out of the mountains into Italy and the western Mediterranean'. It is an uncomfortable reality that, for all his great efforts, Rubau is likely to find the cold dry wind of competition a lot chillier than he expected.

Volkswagen Passat

Design	Hartmut Warkus
Engine	2.0 in-line 4
Power	110 kW (148 bhp) @ 6000 rpm
Torque	200 Nm (147 lb. ft.) @ 3500 rpm
Gearbox	6-speed manual
Installation	Front-engined/front-wheel drive
Front suspension	MacPherson strut
Rear suspension	Multi-link
Brakes front/rear	Discs/discs
Front tyres	205/55R16
Rear tyres	205/55R16
Length	4765 mm (187.6 in.)
Width	1820 mm (71.7 in.)
Height	1472 mm (58 in.)
Wheelbase	2710 mm (106.7 in.)
Track front/rear	1552/1551 mm (61.1/61 in.)
Kerb weight	1389 kg (3062 lb.)
0–100 km/h (62 mph)	9.4 sec
Top speed	213 km/h (132 mph)
Fuel consumption	8.2 l/100 km (34.5 mpg)
CO_2 emissions	197 g/km

Once again the Volkswagen Passat has taken a step up the status ladder. In line with VW's policy of moving its offerings into semi-premium positionings in each market sector, the new, sixth-generation Passat now counts blue-chip models such as the BMW 3 Series and the Mercedes-Benz C-Class as its competitors, rather than volume-segment cars such as the Ford Mondeo and the Opel Vectra.

A shiny new suit of clothes confirms the Passat's premium-sector intentions: the new car has much of the visual allure of the top-luxury Phaeton, especially in the profile of the window line and the D-pillar. A longer wheelbase and the transverse mounting of the engine free up more space for passengers and luggage, again reinforcing the move upmarket.

To make the most of its larger, grander profile, the new Passat is given more surface detailing. Chrome trim runs round the side windows and also low down round the whole car. At the front the chrome grille is very pronounced, extending down to support the number plate. The headlamps have twin circular lenses, the outer one cutting down into the bumper and drawing attention to the front's width. This is becoming VW's favoured front-end signature and was trailed on the Concept R roadster and Concept C coupé-cabriolet shown recently. The lamps at the rear are also very striking, and set twin white lenses into a red lamp, split between the squared-off body corner and the boot face.

Inside, the cabin has the look and feel of luxury, with a wide centre console trimmed in leather and wood, and finely detailed and quality switchgear. Again, the feel is Phaeton-smart – classy but restrained. The previous Passat gave the car business a wake-up call on interior quality – and there is no reason why its 2005 successor should not do so too.

Volvo 3CC

Engine	Electric power from lithium-ion battery
Installation	Front-wheel drive
Front suspension	Double wishbone
Rear suspension	Double wishbone
Brakes front/rear	Discs/discs
Front tyres	215/45ZR18
Rear tyres	215/45ZR18
Length	3899 mm (153.5 in.)
Width	1624 mm (63.9 in.)
Height	1321 mm (52 in.)
0–100 km/h (62 mph)	10 sec
Top speed	137 km/h (85 mph)

Innovation in the form of concept cars has come more naturally to Volvo in recent years. The latest example is the 3CC, which sees the Swedish brand researching a group of customers that might become very important in the future: buyers who want cars with a real individual identity, yet at the same time who want a vehicle with a reduced impact on the environment.

The 3CC's format is that of a compact, coupé-like car with three seats. The rear seat is just wide enough to accommodate one adult or two children but is positioned centrally to allow the upper body to be swept inboard to create a truly striking and aerodynamic exterior design, somewhat reminiscent of an aircraft fuselage.

The two-plus-one seating configuration provides many benefits in addition to aerodynamics: all occupants can see the road ahead, and communication between the three is made easier. The swing-up doors are not strictly necessary to the function of the 3CC but do give the concept the sort of visual appeal that draws crowds at auto shows.

Powered by a zero-emission electric drivetrain, the 3CC demonstrates the major advances made in battery power. On a full charge of the lithium-ion batteries – mounted within the floor 'sandwich' to keep the centre of gravity low – the 3CC's range is more than 300 km (185 miles); it hits 100 km/h (62 mph) in ten seconds, helped by a lightweight carbon-fibre body mounted to a high-strength steel spaceframe. In typical driving conditions, roughly 20% of the energy can be recovered by regenerative braking.

The 3CC has come out of Volvo's think-tank in California as a 'future-proof' vehicle that is able to accept a range of powertrain technologies. It is distinctive and innovative, and could be a good prospect for further development.

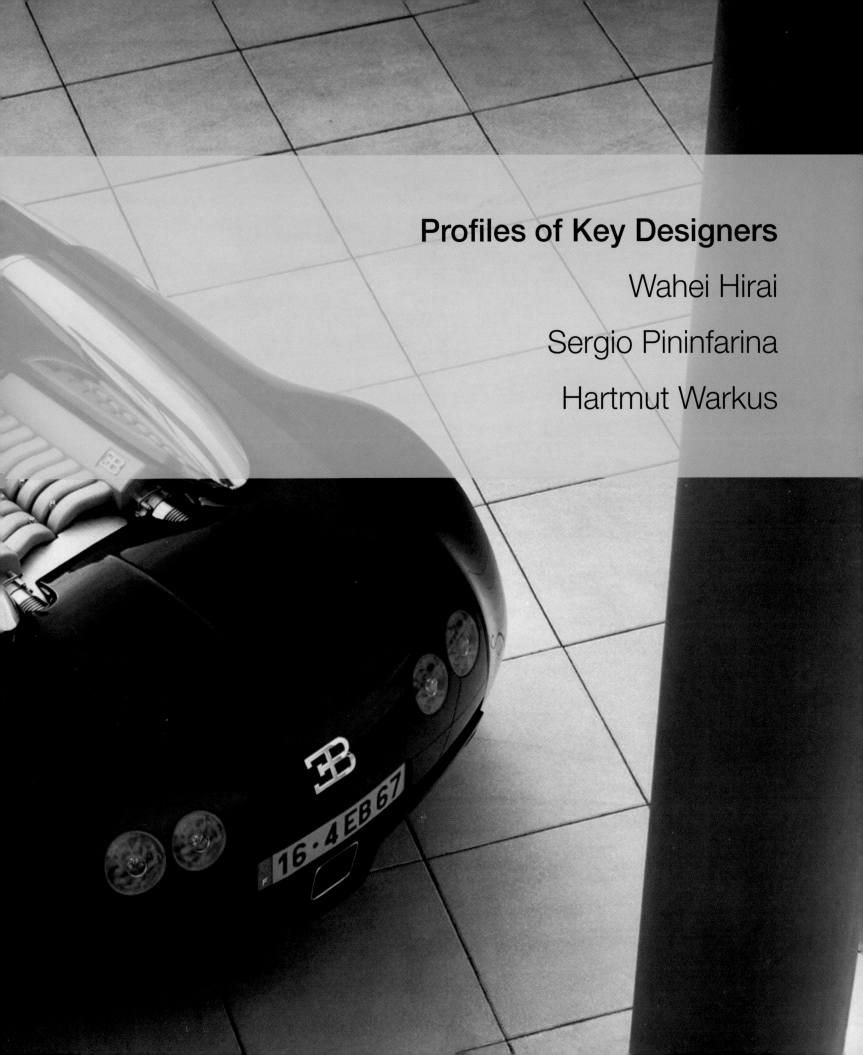

Profiles of Key Designers

Wahei Hirai

Sergio Pininfarina

Hartmut Warkus

Wahei Hirai

Wahei Hirai is a managing officer at Toyota Motor Corporation and head of design and design strategy for both Toyota and Lexus. Born in Tokyo in 1949, and educated at Chiba University, he has spent his entire career at Toyota. Since 1972, when he joined the design department, he has worked his way up through the organization and has worked at Toyota design establishments in Japan, France and the United States.

During the late 1970s, Wahei Hirai led the exterior design of the Celica sports car and the Crown and Cresta saloons. These models soon developed a loyal customer following and were complemented several years later with new-generation models and the addition of the Camry and the Corolla. The designs differed from the models the competition was offering, having many more electrical features and being sold at competitive prices. It was during these years that Toyota's reputation for quality and reliability was being built and consolidated: it should not be underestimated how this fact has played a vital role in keeping customers loyal to the brand.

A more recent landmark in Wahei Hirai's career was the conception of Toyota's new design philosophy, termed 'Vibrant Clarity' – a message first seen on the first-generation Yaris. This hard-to-explain concept is articulated on the Yaris by the desire for it to be perceived not merely as a small and economical car, but also as a car with enjoyable and proud values and its own distinctive character. The Yaris was widely accepted as a ground-breaking new car and, by many, as the best in its class in Europe.

When deciding on the packaging of the Yaris, Hirai's team focused on giving it maximum interior space within a compact exterior. By raising the height of the occupants and moving the A-pillars forward, the designers gained the freedom to think in new ways. For example, the increased dash depth created by the A-pillar's move forward allowed the main instruments to be placed centrally, making a striking symbol in the centre of the instrument panel. The benefits of this were logical in ergonomic as well as visual terms. The increased body height was used to

Opposite top
The 1985 Toyota Celica catapulted Toyota forward in
terms of design. The blackened pillars are treatments
that are still often used today.

Above
The two-tone Toyota Camry from 1987 was a classic
three-box shape, but the focus on strong horizontal lines
and body-coloured bumpers made it look more interesting
than what had come before.

Right
The Yaris has been a huge sales success from launch.
Its innovative packaging and up-to-the-minute looks
helped to make it a winner among strong competition in
the small-car sector.

Wahei Hirai

Above
In 1987 Toyota was offering high-specification interiors loaded with electronics on models like the Corolla, and this, coupled with reliability and a practical package, led to a strong following.

advantage not only for the interior space and visibility but also to create an overall image that was bold and fun, as well as to make the vehicle easier to get into and out of. Other models now exhibiting the design philosophy of Vibrant Clarity are the Prius and the new Scion brand, conveying their concepts in bold, energized forms.

When Toyota launched its upmarket Lexus brand in 1989, the LS400 was widely accepted as a refined and capable car that could challenge the German marques. Lexus now has a firm following. Wahei Hirai's task over the past three years has been to re-evaluate the history and

future of Lexus, a process that has led to the creation of what the company terms 'L-Finesse' – a move towards a more contemporary, dynamic position in the premium market. In design terms this means drawing from Japanese aesthetic values, and results in the creation of a new dynamism based on a visual contrast between simplicity and elegance.

This is how the distinctive new silhouette with the signature Lexus long cabin was born. Quite different from the traditional rear-wheel-drive proportion, it affords a sleek exterior and at the same time a roomy interior, forming the basis for

the GS, the new IS, and future saloon models. The LF-S, shown at the Tokyo Motor Show in 2003, was one of the best examples, and is one of Wahei Harai's personal favourites.

At Toyota today, under Hirai's direction, the role of Toyota's designers is changing rapidly. They are increasingly involved in brand strategy and other corporate design activities in order to ensure that a consistent design message threads its way through all aspects of the company.

In the future, Toyota will be focusing more on conveying a unique identity based on Japanese aesthetic values, known inside Toyota as the 'J-Factor'. The J-Factor focuses not only on traditional values but also on the innovative, energetic side of modern Japanese culture. By building more spirit into the company's designs, Wahei Hirai hopes that Toyota and Lexus design will continue to be appreciated by people from all walks of life, all over the world.

Above
When the Lexus brand was launched in 1989 with the LS400, few thought that a new brand could rival BMW and Mercedes-Benz. But that's what Lexus has achieved by focusing on quality, refinement and reliability.

Sergio Pininfarina

Sergio Pininfarina is in the enviable position of chairing what is probably the most glamorous of all the car design establishments in the world.

Born into the Farina family on 8 September 1926, he graduated in mechanical engineering from the Polytechnic of Turin in 1950 and began his career in the family firm, Carrozzeria Pinin Farina. In 1960 he took responsibility as general manager and in 1966, on his father's death, he took over the chairmanship of the company. The rest, as they say, is history.

During Sergio Pininfarina's fifty-plus years of work, the Pininfarina Group has enjoyed a constant increase in technical and production development; today, with more than 2400 staff and several plants in Italy and abroad, it is widely regarded as the leading design and manufacturing consultancy worldwide.

Sergio Pininfarina has led an illustrious career both within Pininfarina and outside the company. His many roles have included professor of car body design at the Polytechnic of Turin (1974–1977) and member of the European

Parliament (1979–1988). With such passion and enthusiasm for cars, design and business, one wonders how Sergio Pininfarina ever gets time to enjoy his hobbies of golf and sailing. But the real legacy of this dedicated figure is quite simple: the many beautiful and flamboyant cars that have rolled out of the Pininfarina studios and that have made his design company a truly world-class outfit. Some commentators have even dubbed him 'the Michelangelo of the twenty-first century'.

The list of cars that have been designed at Pininfarina is a long one – so we have space to show only a selection of the very finest examples. With Sergio Pininfarina being a member of the board of directors at Ferrari, it is little surprise that several Ferrari models feature here. The Ferrari Dino Speciale prototype in 1965 was the first model for which Sergio can claim responsibility: it arose only after he had succeeded in persuading Enzo Ferrari to adopt what was at that time an unusual mid-engined layout for the car. It was in the creative atmosphere of the Pininfarina Centro Studi e Ricerche in Cambiano that such cars as

Top
The Ferrari F40 of 1987, one of many classics designed by Sergio Pininfarina during a long career.

Opposite top and middle
The 1965 Ferrari Dino Berlinetta Speciale's curves made it a striking-looking car, but the 1984 Ferrari Testarossa must be the most widely recognized Ferrari of all time. The slatted air intakes that run the length of the doors make it immediately identifiable as a Ferrari.

Opposite bottom
The Ferrari Mythos of 1989 is based on a single wedge shape and features an extremely short rear overhang.

Sergio Pininfarina

the Ferrari Testarossa (with its distinctive side-mounted air intakes), the Alfa Romeo Spider, the Ferrari F355 and the 550 Maranello all first saw the light of day. These cars bear out Pininfarina's personal approach to design – the creation of beautiful products that are romantic and exciting, and at the same time functional.

Although Ferrari is Pininfarina's flagship relationship – only eight Ferraris have been designed elsewhere since 1950 – Sergio Pininfarina has played a major role in bringing affordable beauty to the masses, with such models as the Peugeot 406 coupé. There has also been a host of concept cars designed for the French manufacturer, among them the 1971 504 Riviera, the 1976 Peugette, the 1988 405 convertible, and more recently the 1997 Nautilus.

Pininfarina's clients today also include Asian companies such as AviChina, companies that are

looking to reach out into European markets and that see Pininfarina as a safe – as well as imaginative – pair of hands.

As well as having earned state honours and numerous honorary doctorates both in Italy and abroad, Sergio Pininfarina was awarded 'Head of the Century in the International Automotive Hall of Fame' at the 2001 Geneva Motor Show by the German magazine *Auto Welt*, for his unique design creativity.

Although automotive design outsourced to consultancies has taken a dip recently, the Pininfarina organization's remarkable heritage and proven ability to adapt to changing conditions will ensure its lasting success. And it is aided by Sergio Pininfarina's firmly held belief that car shapes can be works of art as enduring as sculpture, and that style as well as steel can resist the corrosive effects of time.

Top
The barrelled sides and flat bonnet of the Ferrari F355 of 1994 made it one of the less extreme Ferrari models, but notably also one of the best-selling.

Above
Pininfarina, which has had a long working relationship with Peugeot, designing many of its niche cars, transformed the 406 coupé of 1996 into a sleek streamlined model.

Opposite top
The Ferrari 550 Maranello was curvaceous, and with a front-engined layout was also more practical than other Ferrari models.

Opposite bottom
A striking design with porthole headlamps and the strong wedge feature makes the Alfa Romeo Spider one of the most recognizable roadsters around.

Hartmut Warkus

For anyone born in Germany in the early stages of the Second World War, life was tough. But for Hartmut Warkus, born on 8 June 1940 in Wroclaw, the first-hand effects of the conflict were doubly tragic: both his father and his younger sister were killed and his remaining family was deported for a period during the latter stages of the war.

The family eventually settled in Solingen, and soon his mother saw the potential in the young Hartmut's drawing skills. When he left school she enrolled him in a training programme to learn the trade of engraving. Not content with this vocation, he followed evening classes in metalwork tooling, which was where his love for three-dimensional forms began to show.

Hartmut's career in the car industry began in 1964 at Mercedes-Benz, where he trained as a designer in the drawing office. It was a key move for the keen young designer, and over the course of the next four decades he went on to work at Ford in Cologne, at Audi in Ingolstadt and finally at Audi's parent company Volkswagen itself,

where he would enjoy a long and influential career until his retirement in 2004.

Warkus's spell at Ford, during which he worked on designs for the Taunus, was relatively brief, and he soon moved on to Audi, where his very first job was to help with the design of the sleek Audi 100 Coupé. The first car that Warkus played a major part in designing was the 1972 Audi 80, a car that marked the beginning of the Audi clean design philosophy that remains today. Next came the Audi 50, a small car that went on to enjoy huge popularity when it became the original Volkswagen Polo.

In 1976 Warkus was appointed head of the Audi Design Centre, and his third-generation Audi 100 proved profoundly influential as the car that ushered in the aerodynamic era. Launched in 1982, the 100 introduced flush glazing for a record-low aerodynamic drag factor of 0.30 – proudly etched on the side windows – and pioneered the smooth, streamlined look that is commonplace today.

Major technical innovations at Audi included

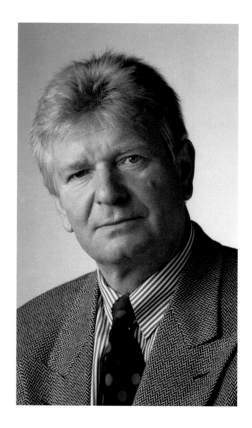

Opposite
The Audi 100 Coupé of 1972.

Right
Audi's clean design philosophy, which began with the Audi 80 of 1972, is still applied today.

Below
The 1997 design of the Audi A8, the world's first all-aluminium mass production car, conveys an impression of space, refinement and practicality.

Hartmut Warkus

the first all-wheel-drive production car, in the shape of the 1980 Audi quattro Coupé and the large A8, the first volume-production all-aluminium car. Warkus maintains that the A8 was his most challenging project as he had to create an original design theme that could compete alongside Mercedes-Benz and Jaguar.

By this time Audi had a firmly established product range that enjoyed a high public profile and was selling well; it was natural that the company would want to demonstrate to the world its design and engineering expertise. This it did by creating several influential show cars, including the Avus, a dramatically proportioned mid-engined supercar finished in polished aluminium, and the neat Audi quattro Spyder.

In 1993 another career move came at the behest of Ferdinand Piëch, who had moved from heading Audi to the chief executive's office of the whole Volkswagen group. Piëch wanted Warkus to accompany him to VW – and his first challenge was to come up with an innovative fifth-generation Passat to stem the flagging sales of the existing model.

The model was a big success and proved to be the first of many that Warkus would produce at Volkswagen. A whole dynasty of big-selling models has been created under the design aegis of Hartmut Warkus: notable examples are the fourth and fifth generations of the iconic Golf, the

Bora, the new Beetle, and the current Polo, Lupo, Phaeton and Touareg.

One of the most adventurous and glamorous projects that Warkus was to oversee was the revival of the famous Bugatti marque. The 400 km/h (250 mph) Veyron may be a far cry from VW's staple diet of mass-market hatchbacks, but it will certainly secure Warkus's place in history as a master of design.

Hartmut Warkus has played a huge role in shaping the modern Volkswagen that we see today – and he can with justification claim some of the credit for VW's pre-eminent position in the European and, increasingly, the world markets of the twenty-first century.

Opposite far left
The mid-engined Audi Avus concept of 1992.

Opposite top right
1991 Audi quattro Spyder

Opposite bottom right
The 1999 Volkswagen Passat had a quality look and was highly practical.

Right
The 2000 Volkswagen Bora is the undemanding quality small saloon for the mass market.

Below
The Bugatti EB 16.4 Veyron from 2000 demonstrates the far-reaching design skill of Hartmut Warkuss.

Technical Glossary

Where the New Models were Launched

Major International Motor Shows 2005–2006

Marques and their Parent Companies

Technical Glossary

Specification tables

The following list explains the terminology used in the specification tables that accompany the model descriptions. The amount of data available for any given model depends on its status as a concept or a production car. More information is usually available for models currently in or nearing production.

Engine	Engine size is quoted in litres, and refers to the swept volume of the cylinders per crankshaft rotation; 6.0, for example, means a 6 litre (or 6000 cc) engine. 'In-line' or 'V' followed by a number refers to the engine's number of cylinders. An in-line 4 engine has four cylinders in a single row, while a V8 engine has eight cylinders arranged in a V-formation. In-line engines of more than six cylinders are rare today because they take up too much packaging space – an in-line 12, for instance, would require a very long bonnet. Only Volkswagen makes a W12, an engine with its twelve cylinders arranged in a W-formation. The configuration of cylinders is usually chosen on cost grounds: the higher the car's retail price, the more cylinders product planners can include.
Power	Engine power is given in both metric kilowatts (kW) and imperial brake horsepower (bhp). Both are calculated at optimum engine crankshaft speed, given in revolutions per minute (rpm) by manufacturers as a 'net' measurement – in other words, an engine's output after power has been sapped by other equipment and the exhaust system – and measured by a 'brake' applied to the driveshaft.
Torque	Simply the motion of twisting or turning, in car terms torque means pulling power, generated by twisting force from the engine crankshaft. It is given in newton metres (Nm) and pounds feet (lb. ft.). The higher the torque, the more force the engine can apply to the driven wheels.
Gearbox	The mechanical means by which power is transmitted from the engine to the driven wheels. There is a wide variety of manual (with a clutch) and automatic (clutchless) versions. There have been recent trends for clutchless manual systems, called 'semi-automatic' or 'automated manual', and automatics with an option to change gear manually, sometimes called 'Tiptronic', 'Steptronic' or 'Easytronic'. 'CVT' (continuously variable transmission) refers to an automatic with a single 'speed': the system uses rubber or steel belts to take engine power to the driven wheels, with drive pulleys that expand and contract to vary the gearing. A 'sequential manual' is a manual gearbox with preset gear ratios that are ordered sequentially.
Suspension	All suspension systems cushion the car against road or terrain conditions to maximize comfort, safety and road holding. Heavy and off-road vehicles use 'rigid axles' at the rear or front and rear; these are suspended using robust, leaf-type springs and steel 'wishbones' with 'trailing arms'. 'Semi-rigid axles' are often found at the back on front-wheel-drive cars, in conjunction with a 'torsion-beam' trailing-arm axle. 'Independent' suspension means each wheel can move up and down on its own, often with the help of 'trailing arms' or 'semi-trailing arms'. A 'MacPherson strut', named after its inventor, a Ford engineer called Earl MacPherson, is a suspension upright, fixed to the car's structure above the top of the tyre. It carries the wheel hub at the bottom and incorporates a hydraulic damper. It activates a coil spring and, when fitted at the front, turns with the wheel.
Brakes	Almost all modern cars feature disc brakes all round. A few low-powered models still feature drum brakes at the back for cost reasons. 'ABS' (anti-lock braking system) is increasingly fitted to all cars: it regulates brake application to prevent the brakes locking in an emergency or slippery conditions. 'BA' (brake assist) is a system that does this electro-hydraulically, while 'EBD' (electronic brake-force distribution) is a pressure regulator that, in braking, spreads the car's weight more evenly so that the brakes do not lock. 'ESP' (electronic stability programme) is Mercedes-Benz's electronically controlled system that helps keep the car pointing in the right direction at high speeds; sensors detect wayward road holding and apply the brakes indirectly to correct it. 'Dynamic stability' is a

similar system. 'Brake-by-wire' is a totally electronic braking system that sends signals from brake pedal to brakes with no mechanical actuation whatsoever. 'TCS' (traction-control system) is a feature that holds acceleration slip within acceptable levels to prevent wheelspin and therefore improves adhesion to the road. 'VSC' (vehicle stability control) is the computer-controlled application of anti-lock braking to all four wheels individually to prevent dangerous skidding during cornering.

Tyres	The size and type of wheels and tyres are given in the internationally accepted formula. Representative examples include: 315/70R17, 235/50VR18, 225/50WR17, 235/40Z18 and 225/40ZR18. In all cases the number before the slash is the tyre width in millimetres. The number after the slash is the height-to-width ratio of the tyre section as a percentage. The letter R denotes radial construction. Letters preceding R are a guide to the tyre's speed rating, denoting the maximum safe operating speed. H tyres can be used at speeds up to 210 km/h (130 mph), V up to 240 km/h (150 mph), W up to 270 km/h (170 mph) and Y up to 300 km/h (190 mph). Finally, the last number is the diameter of the wheel in inches. A 'PAX' is a wheel-and-tyre in one unit, developed by Michelin (for example, 19/245 PAX means a 19 in. wheel with a 245 mm tyre width). The rubber tyre element is clipped to the steel wheel part, rather than held on by pressure. The height of the tyre walls is reduced, which can free up space for better internal packaging, or for bigger wheels for concept car looks. It can also run flat for 200 km at 80 km/h, eliminating the need for a spare.
Wheelbase	The exact distance between the centre of the front wheel and centre of the rear wheel.
Track front/rear	The exact distance between the centre of the front or rear tyres, measured across the car at the ground.
Kerb weight	The amount a car weighs with a tank of fuel, all oils and coolants topped up, and all standard equipment but no occupants.
CO_2 emissions	Carbon dioxide emissions, which are a direct result of fuel consumption. CO_2 contributes to the atmospheric 'greenhouse effect'. Less than 100 g/km is a very low emission, 150 g/km is good, 300 g/km is bad. 'PZEV' (partial zero emission vehicle) refers to a low-level emission standard that was created to allow flexibility on ZEV standards in California.

Other terms

A-, B-, C-, D-pillars	Vertical roof-support posts that form part of a car's bodywork. The A-pillar sits between windscreen and front door, the B-pillar between front and rear doors, the C-pillar between rear doors and rear window, hatchback or estate rear-side windows, and the D-pillar (on an estate) between rear side windows and tailgate. Confusingly, however, some designs refer to the central pillar between front and rear doors as a B-pillar where it faces the front door and a C-pillar where it faces the rear one.
All-wheel drive (AWD)	A system delivering the appropriate amount of engine torque to each wheel via a propshaft and differentials, to ensure that tyre slippage on the road surface is individually controlled. This system is ideal for high-performance road cars, such as Audis, where it's called 'quattro'.
Cant rail	The structural beam that runs along the tops of the doors.
Coefficient of drag	Also known as the Cd, this is shorthand for the complex scientific equation that proves how aerodynamic a car is. The Citroën C-Airdream, for example, has a Cd of 0.28, but the Citroën SM of thirty years ago measured just 0.24, so little has changed in this respect. 'Drag' means the resistance of a body to airflow, and low drag means better penetration, less friction and therefore more efficiency, although sometimes poor dynamic stability.

Diffuser	A custom-designed airflow conduit, often incorporated under the rear floor on high-performance and competition cars, which controls and evenly distributes fast-moving airflow out from beneath the speeding car. This ducting arrangement slows the flow of rushing air behind the car, lowering its pressure and so increasing aerodynamic downforce. The result is improved roadholding.
Drive-by-wire technology	Increasingly featured on new cars, these systems do away with mechanical elements and replace them by wires transmitting electronic signals to activate such functions as brakes and steering.
Drivetrain	The assembly of 'organs' that gives a car motive power: engine, gearbox, driveshaft, wheels, brakes, suspension and steering. This grouping is also loosely known these days as a 'chassis', and can be transplanted into several different models to save on development costs.
Fastback	This refers to the profile of a hatchback that has a rear screen at a shallow angle, so that the tailgate forms a constant surface from the rear of the roof to the very tail end of the car.
Fast windscreen	A windcsreen angled acutely to reduce wind resistance and accentuate a sporty look.
Feature line	A styling detail usually added to a design to differentiate it from its rivals, and generally not related to such functional areas as door apertures.
Four-wheel drive	This refers to a system delivering a car's power to its four wheels. In a typical 'off-road'-type four-wheel-drive vehicle, the differentials can be locked so that all four wheels move in a forward direction even if the tyres are losing grip with the road surface. This makes four-wheel drive useful when travelling across uneven terrain.
Glasshouse/greenhouse	The car-design industry's informal term for the glazed area of the passenger compartment that usually sits above the car's waist level.
Instrument panel	The trim panel that sits in front of the driver and front passenger.
Kamm tail	Sharply cut-off tail that gives the aerodynamic advantages of a much longer, tapering rear end, developed in racing in the 1960s.
Monospace/ monovolume/'one-box'	A 'box' is one of the major volumetric components of a car's architecture. In a traditional saloon, there are three boxes: one for the engine, one for the passengers and one for the luggage. A hatchback, missing a boot, is a 'two-box' car, while a large MPV such as the Renault Espace is a 'one-box' design, also known as a 'monospace' or 'monovolume'.
MPV	Short for 'multi-purpose vehicle', this term is applied to tall, spacious cars that can carry at least five passengers, and often as many as nine, or versatile combinations of people and cargo. The 1983 Chrysler Voyager and 1984 Renault Espace were the first. The 1977 Matra Rancho was the very first 'mini-MPV', but the 1991 Mitsubishi Space Runner was the first in the modern idiom.
Packaging space	Any three-dimensional zone in a vehicle that is occupied by component parts or used during operation of the vehicle.
Platform	Also known as the 'floorpan': the invisible, but elemental and expensive, basic structure of a modern car. It is the task of contemporary car designers to achieve maximum aesthetic diversity from a single platform.
Powertrain	The engine, gearbox and transmission 'package' of a car.

Regenerative braking	When braking in a hybrid electric vehicle, the electric motor that is used to propel the car reverses its action and turns into a generator, converting kinetic energy into electrical power, which is then stored in the car's batteries.
Spaceframe	A structural frame that supports a car's mechanical systems and cosmetic panels.
Splitter	Sometimes found at the front of high-performance cars near to ground level, this is a system of under-car ducting that splits the airflow sucked under the car as it moves forward, so the appropriate volume of cooling air is distributed to both radiator and brakes.
Sub-compact	You need to rewind fifty-four years for the origins: in 1950, Nash launched its Rambler, a two-door model smaller than other mainstream American sedans. The company coined the term 'compact' for it although, by European standards, it was still a large car. Nash's descendant American Motors then invented the 'sub-compact' class in 1970 with the AMC Gremlin, a model with a conventional bonnet and a sharply truncated hatchback tail; this was quickly followed by the similar Ford Pinto and Chevrolet Vega. In the international car industry today, 'sub-compact' is used as another term for 'A-segment', the smallest range of cars, intended mostly for city driving.
SUV	Short for 'sport utility vehicle', a four-wheel-drive car designed for leisure off-road driving but not necessarily agricultural or industrial use. Therefore a Land Rover Defender is not an SUV, while a Land Rover Freelander is. The line between the two is sometimes difficult to draw, and identifying a pioneer is tricky: SUVs as we know them today were defined by Jeep in 1986 with the Wrangler, Suzuki in 1988 with the Vitara, and Daihatsu in 1989 with the Sportrak. There is also a trend towards more sporty trucks, which has led to the more specific term 'SUT', or 'sport utility truck'.
Swage line	A groove or moulding employed on a flat surface to stiffen it against warping or vibration. In cars, swage lines add 'creases' to bodywork surfaces, enabling designers to bring visual, essentially two-dimensional interest to body panels that might otherwise look slab-sided or barrel-like.
Targa	Porsche had been very successful in the Targa Florio road races in Sicily, so, in celebration, in 1965 the company applied the name 'Targa' (the Italian for shield) to a new 911 model that featured a novel detachable roof panel. It is now standard terminology for the system, although a Porsche-registered trademark.
Telematics	Any individual communication to a car from an outside base station; this could be, for example, satellite navigation signals, automatic emergency calls, roadside assistance, traffic information and dynamic route guidance.
Transaxle	Engineering shorthand for 'transmission axle': this is the clutch and gearbox unit that is connected to the driveshafts to transfer power to the driven wheels. All front-wheel-drive and rear- or mid-engined, rear-wheel-drive cars have some type of transaxle.
Venturi tunnel	A venturi is an air-management system under a car designed to increase air speed by forcing it through tapered channels. High air speed creates a low-pressure area between the bottom of the car and the road, which in turn creates a suction effect holding the car to the road. Pressure is then equalized in the diffuser at the rear of the car.

Where the New Models were Launched

New York International Auto Show
9–18 April 2004

Concept
Audi RSQ
Buick Velite
Lexus LF-C

Production
Cadillac STS
Jeep Grand Cherokee
Land Rover
 Discovery/LR3
Nissan Xterra
Saab 9-7X

British Motor Show
28 May – 6 June 2004

Concept
Farboud GTS
Marcos TSO
Noble M14

Production
Opel/Vauxhall Tigra
Renault Modus

Paris Motor Show
25 September –
10 October 2004

Concept
Chevrolet S3X
Etud Intégral Scooto
Ford Focus Vignale
Mercedes-Benz GST
 Vision R
Nissan Tone
Peugeot 907
Peugeot Quark
Pininfarina Double-Face
Pininfarina Nido
Renault Fluence
Sivax Xtile

Production
Audi A4
BMW 1 Series
Citroën C4
Ferrari F430
Ford Focus
Honda FR-V
Hyundai Sonata
Kia Sportage
Mazda 5
Mercedes-Benz A-Class
Opel/Vauxhall Astra GTC
Peugeot 1007
Porsche 911
Porsche Boxster
Seat Toledo
Suzuki Swift

Greater LA Auto Show
7–16 January 2005

Production
Chevrolet HHR
Chevrolet Impala
Pontiac Torrent

North American International Auto Show (NAIAS)
15–23 January 2005

Concept
Acura RD-X
Chrysler Firepower
Ford Explorer Sport Trac
Ford Fairlane
Ford Shelby GR-1
Ford SYNus
GM Sequel
GMC Graphyte
Infiniti Kuraza
Jaguar Advanced
 Lightweight Coupé
Jeep Gladiator
Jeep Hurricane
Kia KCD-II Mesa
Lexus LF-A
Mazda MX-Crossport
Mercury Meta One
Nissan Azeal
Saturn Aura
Suzuki Concept X
Toyota FT-SX
Volvo 3CC

Production
Acura RL
Dodge Charger
Ford Fusion
Honda Ridgeline
Infiniti M
Kia Rio
Lincoln Zephyr
Mercedes-Benz M-Class
Mitsubishi Eclipse
Mitsubishi Raider
Range Rover Sport
Saturn Sky
Subaru B9 Tribeca
Toyota Avalon

Chicago Auto Show
9–20 February 2005

Concept
Dodge Nitro
Honda Civic Si
Hyundai Portico

Production
Buick Lucerne
Cadillac DTS
Dodge Ram Mega-Cab
Hummer H3
Kia Sedona
Mercury Milan
Toyota FJ Cruiser

75th Geneva International Motor Show
3–13 March 2005

Concept
AviChina Hafei Saibao
Bertone Villa
Cadillac BLS
Dodge Caliber
Fenomenon Stratos
Ford SAV
Honda Civic
Italdesign Mitsubishi Nessie
Lamborghini Concept S
Nissan Zaroot
Pininfarina Birdcage 75th
Renault Zoé
Rinspeed Senso
Seat Leon
Skoda Yeti
Stola S86 Diamante
Tata Xover

Production
Alfa Romeo 159
Alfa Romeo Brera
Aston Martin V8 Vantage
BMW 3 Series
Chevrolet Matiz
Citroën C1
Citroën C6
Fiat Croma
Lexus IS
Mazda MX-5
Mercedes-Benz B-Class
Opel/Vauxhall Zafira
Peugeot 107
Toyota Aygo
Tramontana
Volkswagen Passat

Major International Motor Shows 2005–2006

Prague Auto Show
6–10 October 2005
Prague Exhibition Grounds, Prague, Czech Republic
www.incheba.cz

Budapest Motor Show
22–30 October 2005
HUNGEXPO Budapest Fair Centre, Budapest, Hungary
www.automobil.hungexpo.hu

Tokyo Motor Show
22 October – 6 November 2005
Nippon Centre, Makuhari, Chiba, Tokyo, Japan
www.tokyo-motorshow.com

Riyadh Motor Show
23–27 November 2005
Riyadh Exhibition Centre, Riyadh, Saudi Arabia
www.recexpo.com

Middle East International Motor Show
12–16 December 2005
Dubai World Trade Centre, Dubai, United Arab Emirates
www.dubaimotorshow.com

Greater LA Auto Show
6–15 January 2006
Los Angeles Convention Center, Los Angeles, USA
www.laautoshow.com

Brussels International Motor Show
12–22 January 2006
Brussels Expo, Brussels, Belgium
www.salonauto.be

North American International Auto Show (NAIAS)
14–22 January 2006
Cobo Exhibition Center, Detroit, USA
www.naias.com

Chicago Auto Show
9–19 February 2006
McCormick Place South, Chicago, USA
www.chicagoautoshow.com

Canadian International Auto Show
Dates not yet available
Metro Toronto Convention Center and SkyDome, Toronto, Canada
www.autoshow.ca

Melbourne International Motor Show
9–19 February 2006
Melbourne Exhibition Centre, Melbourne, Australia
www.motorshow.com.au

Geneva International Motor Show
2–12 March 2006
Palexpo, Geneva, Switzerland
www.salon-auto.ch

British International Motor Show
20–30 July 2006
Excel, London, UK
www.britishmotorshow.co.uk

Frankfurt International Motor Show
17–25 September 2006
Trade Fairgrounds, Frankfurt am Main, Germany
www.iaa.de

Paris Motor Show
30 September – 15 October 2006
Paris Expo, Paris, France
www.mondialauto.tm.fr

Marques and their Parent Companies

Hundreds of separate car-making companies have consolidated over the past decade into ten groups: General Motors, Ford, DaimlerChrysler, VW, Toyota, Peugeot, Renault, BMW, Honda and Hyundai. These account for at least nine of every ten cars produced globally today. The remaining independent marques either produce specialist models, offer niche design and engineering services or tend to be at risk because of their lack of economies of scale. The global over-capacity in the industry means that manufacturers are having to offer increased choice to the consumer to differentiate their brands and maintain market share. Not all parent companies fully own the car-makers listed as under their control. Subaru, for example, operates within the General Motors alliance but is only 21% owned by the US giant.

BMW
BMW
Mini
Riley*
Rolls-Royce
Triumph*

DaimlerChrysler
Chrysler
De Soto*
Dodge
Hudson*
Imperial*
Jeep
Maybach
Mercedes-Benz
Nash*
Plymouth*
Smart

Fiat Auto
Abarth*
Alfa Romeo
Autobianchi*
Ferrari
Fiat
Innocenti*
Lancia
Maserati

Ford
Aston Martin
Daimler*
Ford
Jaguar
Lagonda*
Land Rover/
  Range Rover
Lincoln
Mazda
Mercury
Th!nk
Volvo

General Motors
Buick
Cadillac
Chevrolet
Corvette
Daewoo
GM
GMC
Holden
Hummer
Isuzu
Oldsmobile*
Opel
Pontiac
Saab
Saturn
Subaru
Suzuki
Vauxhall

Honda
Acura
Honda

Hyundai
Asia Motors
Hyundai
Kia

MG Rover
Austin*
MG*
Morris*
Rover*
Wolseley*

PSA-Peugeot
Citroën
Citroën
Hillman*
Humber*
Panhard*
Peugeot
Simca*
Singer*
Sunbeam*
Talbot*

Proton
Lotus
Proton

Renault-Nissan
Alliance
Alpine*
Dacia
Datsun*
Infiniti
Nissan

Renault
Renault Sport
Samsung

Toyota
Daihatsu
Lexus
Scion
Toyota
Will*

Volkswagen
Group
Audi
Auto Union*
Bentley
Bugatti
Cosworth
DKW*
Horch*
Lamborghini
NSU*
Seat
Skoda
Volkswagen
Wanderer*

Independent
marques
Austin-Healey*
AviChina
Beijing
Bertone
Bristol
Byd
Caterham
Chery
Dongfeng
Donkervoort
EDAG
Elfin
Etud Intégral
Farboud
Fenomenon
Fioravanti
Heuliez
Hindustan
Invicta
Irmscher
Italdesign
Izh
Jensen
Joss
Koenigsegg
Lada
Mahindra

Marcos
Maruti
Mitsubishi
Mitsuoka
Morgan
Pagani
Panoz
Paykan
Perodua
Pininfarina
Porsche
Rinspeed
Sivax
Spyker
SsangYong
Stola
Tata
Tramontana
TVR
Venturi
Volga
Westfield
Wiesmann
Zagato
ZAZ
ZIL

* Dormant
marques

Acknowledgements

I would like to thank everyone involved at Merrell Publishers for the continuing success of the *Car Design Yearbook* series, in particular Marion Moisy, Nicola Bailey, Kirsty Seymour-Ure, John Grain, Michelle Draycott and Anthea Snow. Thanks are due to Tony Lewin for his editorial support and to Alistair Layzell for the publicity campaign.

Thanks are also due to the manufacturers' press offices for providing the photographs for the book. Final thanks go to my fiancée, Hannah James-Roll.

Stephen Newbury
Henley-on-Thames, Oxfordshire
2005

Picture Credits

The illustrations in this book have been reproduced with the kind permission of the following manufacturers and sources:

Alfa Romeo
Aston Martin Lagonda
Audi AG
Bertone
BMW AG
Chevrolet
Citroën
DaimlerChrysler
Dodge
EDAG
Etud Intégral
Farboud
Fenomenon
Fiat Auto
Ford Motor Company
General Motors Corporation
Honda Motor Co.

Hyundai Car UK
Italdesign
Jaguar Cars
Kia Motors Corporation
Lamborghini
Land Rover
Lincoln
Marcos
Mazda Motors
Mitsubishi Motors Corporation
Nissan Motors
Noble
Opel AG
Peugeot SA
Pininfarina SpA
Pontiac
Porsche

Renault SA
Rinspeed
Saab Automobile AB
Saturn
Seat SA
Skoda
Sivax
Stola
Subaru
Suzuki Motor Corporation
Tata Motors
Tramontana
Toyota Motor Corporation
Volkswagen AG
Volvo Car Corporation

Giles Chapman Library

301

MERRELL

First published 2005 by Merrell Publishers Limited

Head office
81 Southwark Street
London SE1 0HX
Telephone +44 (0)20 7928 8880
E-mail mail@merrellpublishers.com

New York office
49 West 24th Street, 8th floor
New York, NY 10010
Telephone +1 212 929 8344
E-mail info@merrellpublishersusa.com

www.merrellpublishers.com

Publisher Hugh Merrell
Editorial Director Julian Honer
US Director Joan Brookbank
Sales and Marketing Manager Kim Cope
Sales and Marketing Executive Nora Kamprath
Managing Editor Anthea Snow
Project Editor Claire Chandler
Junior Editor Helen Miles
Art Director Nicola Bailey
Junior Designer Paul Shinn
Production Manager Michelle Draycott
Production Controller Sadie Butler

British Library Cataloguing-in-Publication data:
Newbury, Stephen
The car design yearbook 4 : the definitive annual
guide to all new concept and production cars
worldwide
1.Automobiles – Periodicals 2.Automobiles –
Design – Periodicals
I.Title
629.2'22'05

ISBN 1 85894 285 3

Consultant editor: Tony Lewin
Project managed by Marion Moisy
Edited by Kirsty Seymour-Ure
Proof-read by Barbara Roby
Designed by John Grain
Design concept by Kate Ward

Printed and bound in China

Frontispiece: Jaguar Advanced Lightweight Coupé
Pages 4–5: Volvo 3CC
Pages 8–9: Saab 9-7X
Pages 22–23: Aston Martin V8 Vantage
Pages 34–35: Land Rover Discovery/LR3
Pages 278–79: Bugatti Veyron
Pages 292–93: Ford Explorer Sport Trac
Pages 302–303: Mazda MX-5